This publication has been produced on behalf of RAC by Veloce Publishing Ltd.

The views and the opinions expressed by the author are entirely his own, and do not necessarily reflect those of the RAC.

First published in October 2010 by Veloce Publishing Limited, Veloce House, Parkway Farm Business Park, Middle Farm Way, Poundbury, Dorchester, Dorset, DT1 3AR, England.
Tel 01305 260068. Fax 01305 250479. email info@veloce.co.uk

ISBN: 978-1-845843-50-2 UPC: 6-36847-04350-6

Readers with ideas for automotive books, or books on other transport or related hobby subjects, are invited to write to the editorial director of Veloce Publishing at the above address.

British Library Cataloguing in Publication Data – A catalogue record for this book is available from the British Library.

Typesetting, design and page make-up all by Veloce Publishing Ltd on Apple Mac.

Printed in India by Imprint Digital Ltd.

Roads with a View

England's greatest views and
how to find them by road

VELOCE PUBLISHING
THE PUBLISHER OF FINE AUTOMOTIVE BOOKS

David Corfield

Contents

Foreword

We all love to moan about the state of our roads, but in making *Roads with a View* I have been reminded of the great treasures that lie at the end of many of them. England is rich in great places – from stunning coastland to magnificent mountain views – and if you're willing to brave a few potholes and the occasional traffic jam – as I have – I can guarantee you will not be disappointed.

I'll see you out there!
Best wishes

David Corfield
Tixover

Acknowledgements

I must extend my heartfelt thanks to Rod, Jude, Paul and Hatty at Veloce for sharing my vision and rolling up their collective sleeves to make *Roads with a View* a reality. Of course, this book would be nothing without stunning images, and I am also very grateful indeed for the kind contributions made by photographers Tom Mackie, Rod Edwards, Ross Hoddinott, and Andrew Dunn.

The author would like to thank the following contributors for their expert advice, patience and guidance in compiling routes and area information: Ferne Arfin, About.com guide to UK Travel, Keswick Tourism Association, Simon Davies from Mysterious Britain, James McCartney, Alnwick Tourist Information, Daniel Parkinson, John Howes for his expert advice on the Malvern Hills, Ashley Thompson, Enjoy England, Nicholas Roe, Thaxted Council, Karen Hodgson on all matters Lincoln and, last but by no means least, the Norfolk Tourism Team. Thank you all for your kind help!

For Laura. May all my roads lead me to you

Lake District & Northumberland

Wastwater

Britain's deepest – and coldest – lake, Wastwater is legend among landscapes as both unforgiving, yet alluring. A visit to the Lake District would not be complete without seeing it

Driving the narrow road that hugs the western shore of Wastwater, you just can't help but be impressed by the mountains that mass and plunge steeply into the lake along the eastern shore. England's deepest lake – diving 15.24 metres (50 feet) below sea level from a surface of at least 61m (200ft) above sea level – sits at the foot of Scafell Pike; at 978 metres (3209 feet), England's highest mountain, but still only one of the giants towering above Wastwater. Other giants include Scafell (964m/3163ft), Great End (910m/2986ft), Bow Fell (901m/2959ft), Great Gable (899m/2949ft), Fell Kirk (820m/2691ft), and Pillar (892m/2926ft). Mountains hovering around the 915 metres (3000 feet) mark may not seem like much compared to the Alps, but the open bulk of the Lake District peaks and their bleak, treeless aspect make Wastwater a truly awe-inspiring place.

There is a rumour that a Lancaster bomber lies 77 metres (252 feet) down in the lake, towards the Wasdale Head Inn end. The story has been taken so seriously that several technical divers have been down looking for it, and it's even appeared on some aircraft heritage website forums. However, there are no records of a Lancaster crashing into Wastwater, and the person who is said to have found it has since moved abroad. The mystery continues …

Directions to Wastwater
Wasdale Head is reached from the main A595. From the south, turn right at Holmrook for Santon Bridge and follow signs to Wasdale Head. From the north, turn left at Gosforth
Please see map on following page

Best food/drink
Wasdale Head Inn, Wasdale Head, Near Gosforth, Cumbria CA20 1EX
Tel: 019467 26229

Wastwater is, perhaps, Cumbria's least visited lake, but its beauty is undeniable when shot at late evening with the mighty silhouettes of the mountains adding to its impact.

Ashness Bridge

One of the most photographed bridges in England, the appeal of Ashness Bridge and the views it affords are timeless to all who visit

It's what many photographers call a 'biscuit tin' scene, as it's traditional and cannot be aged. Ashness Bridge has been standing for centuries, and doubtless will be around for quite a few more yet.

Take a trip south of Keswick along the B5289, which winds along the shores of Derwentwater, offering magnificent views across the lake to Catbells and Maiden Moor. The National Trust Great Wood car park will give you an opportunity to leave the car and stroll down to the lake shore through the woods – a perfect excuse to get your feet wet!

A mile or so further on and a minor road branches off steeply to the left, leading to Watendlath over and past Ashness Bridge. This fine, small bridge, straddling a fast running beck, is a perfect foreground for the view north over Derwentwater and Bassenthwaite, with the mass of the Skiddaw Peak rising steeply above Keswick. Even more dramatic is the Surprise View panorama a little further up the hill overlooking Keswick and Derwentwater.

The narrow, wall-rimmed lane twists its way along a 'hidden' valley to the hamlet of Watendlath, home of Judith Paris, a character in the novels by Hugh Walpole. Park in the car parks at Surprise View and enjoy the easy two-and-a-half mile walk to Watendlath; there's a footpath along the other side of the river for the return journey, if you have appropriate footwear. The hamlet has a seven-acre tarn of the same name, stocked with trout for fishing.

Watendlath is entirely owned and protected by the National Trust, as are many of the farms, much of the lake, and most of the surrounding fells in the Borrowdale Valley. The minor road comes to an end in Watendlath, and beyond this a path leads up into the fells and over and down into Rosthwaite.

Back on the B5289, just past the attractive village of Grange in Borrowdale, with its double-arched bridge, a short walk from a car park leads to the Bowder Stone, a massive fallen rock. The stone can be climbed by ladder and is perched in such a way that hands can be joined underneath its 2000 ton bulk. The chalky marks on the sides of the stone show the handholds of 'boulderers' who have tried to climb the overhang.

The main Borrowdale valley road then winds along beside the River Derwent to the traditional Lakeland villages of Rosthwaite and Seatoller. Then Honister Pass rises steeply up to Honister slate mine at the summit, a working mine and popular visitor attraction.

If you need a rest from driving, why not try the local bus service? The Borrowdale Rambler operates all year round, and goes from Keswick as far as Seatoller at the head of the Borrowdale Valley. Operating during the summer season only, the Honister Rambler takes in Borrowdale, the spectacular Honister Pass, Buttermere, the Lorton Valley, and Whinlatter. Explorer tickets are available for one or more days, so you can hop on and off as you wish. To visit Ashness Bridge via public transport, take the Borrowdale bus service (number 79) and get off at the Derwentwater Youth Hostel stop. From there, it's only a short stroll up the lane to the bridge and along a footpath to Surprise View. If you want a longer walk, it's about 4km to the hamlet of Watendlath with its tarn and cafe.

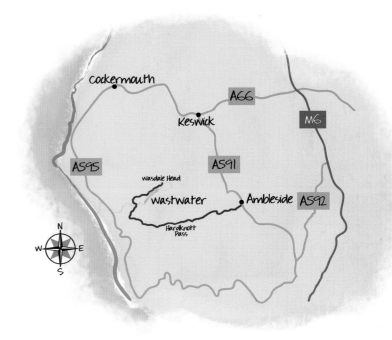

Ashness Bridge is one of the Lake District's jewels, affording stunning views over Derwentwater, with the bustling town of Keswick a short drive away.

Directions to Ashness Bridge
Drive south from Keswick along Derwentwater, and take a small, steep turning on the left after 4 kilometres (2.4 miles) signed to Ashness Bridge

Best food/drink
Bank Tavern, 47 Main Street, Keswick, Cumbria CA12 5DS
Tel: 017687 72663

Relevant websites
http://www.beerintheevening.com/
pubs/s/13/13052/Bank_Tavern/Keswick

Langdale Valley; Hardknott and Wrynose Passes

The author's home for much of his childhood can still be relied upon to spring a few surprises

Few roads in England offer such a dramatic blend of breathtaking views and great tarmac in such a short radius. The Lake District is certainly one of these places, despite the rush of summer traffic to the hotspots of Windermere and Coniston.

But stray from the crowds and Cumbria still throws up plenty of surprises, none more delightful than the Langdale Valley, and its Hardknott and Wrynose passes.

Both routes offer superb scenery, but do need care if you want to stop and grab a quick shot. Always keep a keen eye in the rear-view mirror before coming to a halt – and that's just as important on the way up as it is on the way down!

Both Hardknott and Wrynose are single-track roads, running right through the middle of the Lake District. Steep, twisting, and great fun when the weather is right, they demand a lot from you as a driver but offer a lot of rewards in return. Amazingly, the roads only got their first taste of tarmac after the Second World War, when they were used as tank training routes. They'd previously been just dirt tracks!

Hardknott Pass carries the minor road between Eskdale and the Duddon Valley. Wrynose Pass then continues, taking the road to the Langdale Valley, and then on to Ambleside.

The Hardknott Pass vies with Rosedale Chimney in North Yorkshire for the title of steepest road in England, both achieving a gradient of 1-in-3 (about 33 per cent).

Hardknott Fort (known to the Romans as Mediobogdum) is near the Eskdale end of Hardknott Pass. The fort, one of the loneliest outposts of the Roman Empire, was built between AD120 and AD138, and lies on a spectacular site overlooking the pass that forms part of the Roman road from Ravenglass to Ambleside.

The Wrynose Pass reaches an altitude of 393m or 1281 feet. The descent into the Duddon Valley, or Wrynose Bottom, is an unremitting sequence of steep hairpin bends, but the view in front is quite stunning. Wrynose Bottom opening up before you, with the Hardknott Pass in the distance. On the return journey up this section, a decidedly uneasy feeling is experienced as you lose sight of the road below the line of the bonnet from time to time, whilst picking your way through the hairpins. Instead of the usual need to observe what is happening in front, it's sometimes necessary to try and anticipate what is going on barely

Spot the road! Early morning mist rises from the valley floor.

13

an inch to your right and four inches above you, as the road winds through the tight bends.

After descending to Wrynose Bottom, the road – still relatively narrow – meanders alongside the River Duddon. To the right, a footpath runs parallel with the road; this is the remains of the old Roman Road. If you come here very early in the morning, you will get a real sense of solitude, but later in the day the road gets very busy, partly because it's the only link from the central lakes to the west coast, but also because of the notoriety of both passes, and drivers' determination to test themselves and the nerves of their passengers!

At the top of the Wrynose Pass is the Three Shire Stone, marking the meeting point of the historic counties of Cumberland, Lancashire and Westmorland.

Directions to Langdale, Wrynose and Hardknott Passes
The A593 Ambleside-Coniston and B5343 both pass close by. Minor roads then lead into Little Langdale Valley on the way to the Wrynose and Hardknott Passes, or, take the road towards Great Langdale, via the Blea Tarn Pass (both routes are steep and narrow in places)

Best food/drink
The New Dungeon Ghyll Hotel, Great Langdale, Ambleside, Cumbria LA22 9JY
Tel: 08721 077077

Relevant websites
http://en.wikipedia.org/wiki/Three_Shire_Stone_ (Lake_District
http://en.wikipedia.org/wiki/Historic_counties_of_ England
http://en.wikipedia.org/wiki/Cumberland
http://en.wikipedia.org/wiki/Lancashire
http://en.wikipedia.org/wiki/Westmorland

Langdale Valley.

Hartside Pass

The A686 – known as Hartside Pass – is one of the UK's best driving roads. If visiting the north of England, this is a route you really have to do!

The Hartside Pass in Cumbria links the villages of Melmerby and Alston. The A686 road climbs the Hartside Pass to a height of 590 metres making it a spectacular drive as you ascend into the North Pennines. At the top there are magnificent views across the Solway Firth to Scotland. The road continues to the town of Alston, England's highest market town.

Located between Penrith and Alston at the summit of Hartside Pass is the Hartside Top Café, From the viewpoint at the café, you can see Helvellyn, Great Gable, Skiddaw, and, in southern Scotland, Criffel. The views really are amazing.

The Pass itself, up to the summit, is a rollercoaster ride of twists and turns, with several hairpins. It's very difficult to explain just how good this road is, but let's put it this way: it is breathtaking, and once the climb to the summit is made, you pull into the Hartside Top Café, where a great variety of food and drink is available. Be warned, though; it isn't the cheapest place on earth, though it is good quality!

Directions to Hartside Pass
At the A66 Penrith roundabout take the third exit and join the A686 heading toward Alston: *this* is the Hartside Pass!

Best food/drink
Hartside Top Café, Alston, Cumbria CA9 3BW
Tel: 01434 381036

Relevant websites
http://www.visitcumbria.com/pen/alston.htm
http://www.visitcumbria.com/pen/a686.htm
http://www.visitcumbria.com/pen/alston.htm
http://www.visitcumbria.com/pen/melmerby.htm

The road by Buttermere Fell, Cumbria.

Northumberland

If it's wide-open spaces, superb views, and great roads you're looking for, they don't get much better than this!

Northumberland is the most sparsely populated county in England, with just 62 people per square kilometre. It's also the site of many historic battles, with several magnificent castles dotted along its coast and further inland.

Alnwick (pronounced 'Annick') and its castle, are perhaps best known in recent years for being the location of 'Hogwarts' in the Harry Potter films, and the town marks the gateway to some of the most unspoilt parts of the county, offering drivers some excellent stretches of road to enjoy whilst passengers admire the stunning scenery.

From Alnwick, head uphill through the centre, and take the B6341 heading to Rothbury, 11 miles away. Immediately the road begins to climb, and continues to rise above sea level for about three miles. At the summit of the hill there is a layby where you can stop and take in the view. And what a view: from here you can see in superb panorama the whole of the Northumberland coastline from Blyth in the south and north east towards the Farne Islands. Crane your neck northwest and you will see the rolling Cheviot Hills in the distance.

Continue your drive and, after half a mile or so, the road bears left, everything on the right dropping away to give a clear and unobstructed view of the Cheviot and sister hills. This is one of the best views in England. There are parking areas a little further on the right, but be careful you don't go too near the edge!

This is a perfect photo opportunity, and probably one of the most spectacular views in Northumberland. From here you can see the Victorian railway viaduct at Edlingham, beyond which is the medieval castle dating from the 14th century and a small church which is said to date back to Saxon times. A short stroll downhill from the parking area brings you to a small bridge over a stream, behind which on the left-hand side of the road, is a lovely waterfall, best seen after heavy rain.

Continue your drive towards Rothbury and you will cross a main road, the A697. Three miles further on you will arrive at the National Trust's Cragside Estate, a fantastic property that is really well worth stopping for. As you get to the bottom of the hill you will see Tumbleton lake and the Cragside stable block above it: this is now the visitor centre for the estate. A little further on is Rothbury, a small, bustling market town (ironically, now without a market!), but still with a good range of shops, as well as a good variety of places to eat.

A recommendation of where to eat here is Harley's Tea Rooms in Bridge Street. Park in the main car park just over the bridge and walk back over the road bridge. The Ridley family will make you very welcome and offer you good, old-fashioned, friendly table service and fine quality food.

After your refreshment continue your drive west along the main street through Rothbury and follow the signs for Otterburn, approximately 14 miles away. As you leave Rothbury behind you can't help but notice the massive range of hills on the left; these are the Simonside Hills, made famous in Anya Seaton's novel, *Devil's Water*.

The river on your left is the Coquet (pronounced 'coke-it'), and the next village you will drive through is Thropton. The Three Wheat Heads Pub in Thropton has gained a reputation for good food. Continue straight through the village and the Coquet-dale opens out into a wide valley. After a few miles you will see a small caravan park on the right-hand side as you begin ascend a steep hill; this is Billsmoorfoot (or Bills Moor Foot). The high stone wall on your left encloses a deer park comprising a herd of Fallow deer. When you get to the top of the hill you will find a parking area and viewpoint on your left; you may be lucky (with the aid of binoculars) to catch a glimpse of the herd as it grazes under the trees.

The next village you come to is Elsdon. Just as you cross the bridge you will see a 13th century Pele tower on your right, which is still lived in today. Pele towers were places of refuge during the many raids by the Border Reivers; another reminder of this county's heritage.

Continue on toward Otterburn, turning right onto the A696. As you approach Otterburn, look out for signs on your left for Kielder Water and Bellingham; follow the signs for Bellingham and the B6320. Bellingham is a lovely little town with a small range of shops and pubs: although small, it is the largest inhabited area for miles. On the edge of Bellingham there is a lovely walk to a waterfall, if you have the time – look out for the signpost. Continue through Bellingham for Kielder and, after a few more miles, you will come to the Pheasant Inn at Stannersburn – another lovely place to eat! Just beyond the village you will arrive at Kielder Water, the largest man-made lake in Europe, where there are walks, picnic places, and boat cruises to enjoy if you have the time.

Making your way home now, continue driving along the shore of Kielder Water, eventually arriving at Kielder Village with its castle. From here you can pick up the forest drive on a gravel road of about 11 miles. Continue along the drive until you exit onto the A68. Turn right onto the A68 towards Otterburn (signed for Newcastle), and eventually the A68 becomes the A696. Travel through Otterburn and look for the B6341 road (signposted Rothbury) on the left. Retrace your steps to Rothbury, and then back to Alnwick.

Following page: Pauperhaugh lies a few miles outside Rothbury, on the River Coquet. The bridge is made of the type of stone that is typical of many bridges in northern England. This one is Grade II listed and is still in use today.

Dunstanburgh Castle lies on a headland between the villages of Craster and Embleton. The largest castle in Northumberland, it was a favourite of the painter Turner, who used to rise at dawn to paint it in the early morning light.

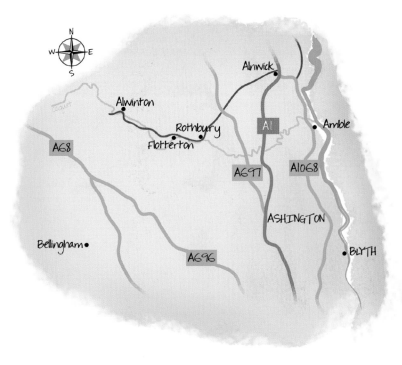

Directions to Alnwick
From Newcastle, take the A1 north towards Alnwick, then the A1068 west to the town centre

Best food/drink
Queens Head Hotel, 25 Market Street, Alnwick, Northumberland NE66 1SS
Tel: 01665 604691

Relevant websites
www.nationaltrust.org.uk/main/w-vh/w-visits/w-findaplace/w-cragsidehousegardenandestate/
www.harleystearoom.co.uk/about.html
www.thepheasantinn.com/
www.visitnorthumberland.com/site/highlights/the-icons/kielder-water-and-forest-park

Alnwick Castle rises from the town in floodlit majesty. Used in the Harry Potter films, it's a great place to visit for all the family – but especially kids, who will love looking for Harry amongst its many nooks and crannies!

Bamburgh Castle

Standing on a rocky outcrop overlooking miles of beautiful sandy beach, Bamburgh Castle dominates the Northumbrian landscape

There's something magically romantic about castles, and perhaps the best example of this is Bamburgh.

The castle became the passion of the first Baron Armstrong, engineer and industrialist, who, in the 1890s, began its renovation and refurbishment. This love of Bamburgh was passed down through the family to the late Lord Armstrong, who personally oversaw the completion of his ancestor's dream.

Today, Bamburgh Castle is still the home of the Armstrong family, and visitors are able to enjoy what has been described as the finest castle in all of England. The public tour includes the magnificent King's Hall, the Cross Hall, reception rooms, the Bakehouse and Victorian scullery, as well as the armoury and dungeon. Throughout, these rooms contain a wide range of fine china, furniture, tapestries, arms and armour.

But it's perhaps the views from the sands that are the best reward, particularly at dawn when the sun rises over the sea. A favourite of many landscape photographers, the view continues to inspire – as you will discover when you visit!

Directions to Bamburgh Castle
Bamburgh Castle is situated 42 miles north of Newcastle-upon-Tyne and 20 miles south of Berwick-upon-Tweed. Take the B1342 from the A1 at Belford to Bamburgh

Best food/drink
Bamburgh Castle Inn, Seahouses, Northumberland NE68 7SQ
Tel: 01665 720283

Relevant websites
http://en.wikipedia.org/wiki/Craster
http://en.wikipedia.org/wiki/Embleton,_
Northumberland

Bamburgh is one of the most beautiful castles in the whole of England, and well worth a trip to Northumberland. Stunning coastline, too!

The Cotswolds

The Cotswolds

Until a few years ago, the broad, smooth road between Northampton and Banbury was identified as the B4525. Most of it is now classified as a lane, which explains why very little traffic uses what could be mistaken for an A road.

This hidden highway starts in Kislingbury, just off the A45 that links Northampton to the M1. Busy main roads are forgotten while cruising across the green and gently undulating heart of England, heeding 'Badgers crossing' signs and admiring old buildings of beautifully weathered stone. Navigation is easy, as long as you bear right in Bugbrooke, following the sign for Litchborough, and take care when crossing the A5.

Canons Ashby House, now owned by the National Trust, is one of several fine properties hidden away in this area of unspoiled land between Northampton, Brackley, Banbury and Daventry. Sulgrave Manor, reached by a short, well-signed detour, belies its off-the-beaten-track location by welcoming many visitors from America (George Washington's ancestors lived here before crossing the Atlantic).

Brace yourself for a brief return to the real world, because you'll soon cross the M40 and crawl through the traffic of Banbury. The Victorian version of the town's famous cross stands on a roundabout where the B4035 begins its 30 mile run over the Cotswolds to Evesham, with the Malvern Hills rising in the distance.

Broughton Castle, in the first of several villages, has been inhabited ever since it was built as a fortified manor house 700 years ago. Owners have included William of Wykeham, who founded Winchester School and New College, Oxford. The B4035 also passes Swalcliffe's handsome tithe barn, which houses vintage agricultural machinery. A few miles later, there are extensive views from Oxfordshire's border with Warwickshire, where the road rises to nearly 213 metres (700 feet).

Follow the B4035 through Shipston-on-Stour and over the Foss Way to Chipping Campden. There's plenty to see here, so park the car and stretch your legs in one of England's loveliest towns. The must-see list includes the parish church, where exquisite marble effigies of Sir Baptist Hicks and his wife are watched over by a statue of Sir Edward Noel, who was killed fighting for the Royalists in the Civil War.

Sir Baptist built Campden House, next to the church. It was burned during the Civil War, but buildings which escaped include a delightful banqueting house, now leased to the Landmark Trust and available for self-catering holidays.

The High Street has an eye-catching Market Hall, and such tempting shops as Bennett's Fine Wines. Pubs abound, of course, but our straw poll of locals gave top marks to the 14th century Eight Bells, a few paces from the church.

At the west end of Lower Slaughter there is an old water mill with an undershot waterwheel, and a chimney for additional steam power.

This is where we briefly desert the B4035, driving along the High Street and reaching Dover's Hill, a spectacular viewpoint, by keeping straight ahead at the crossroads on the outskirts of Chipping Campden. Part of the Cotswolds' steep escarpment, Dover's Hill is where Captain Robert Dover's famous 'Olympick Games,' which included such events as shin kicking, were staged every Whitsun from 1612 until 1852.

There's a change of mood and pace, as we plunge down to rejoin the B4035 as it reaches the Vale of Evesham, flicking left and right through Weston-sub-Edge. The route skirts Bretforton, but a left turn reveals a village notable for the medieval Fleece Inn. Henry Byrd began selling beer and cider here in 1848. His great-granddaughter, Lola Taplin, pulled pints until she died in 1977, and left the pub to the National Trust.

At journey's end, three miles later, traffic on the Evesham bypass comes as a shock after crossing so much of central England on blissfully quiet B roads.

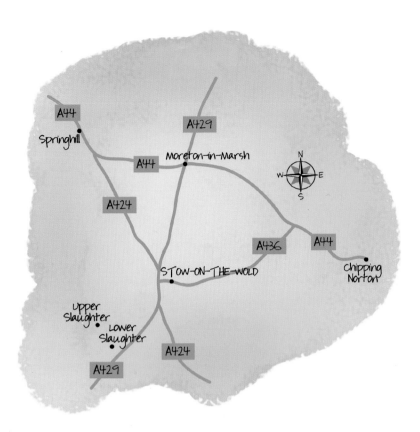

Directions to Lower Slaughter
Take the M40 north, exiting at junction 8. Follow the A40 to Oxford and Burford. Turn right at the roundabout into Burford. At the bottom of the hill turn left onto the A424 Stow Road. After about 8 miles turn left at the traffic lights onto the A429. In 1 mile turn right into the Slaughters

Best food/drink
Queens Head Inn, The Square, Stow on the Wold, Cheltenham GL54 1AB
Tel: 01451 830563

Relevant websites
http://en.wikipedia.org/wiki/Water_mill
http://en.wikipedia.org/wiki/Waterwheel

Directions to Little Barrington

 Head to Burford on the A40, and drive past the town to Upton. Join the B4425 and Little Barrington is a pleasant couple of miles' drive along this road

Little Barrington is a very picturesque Cotswold village with a lot of history. Thomas Strong from Barrington was considered the finest stonemason of his time, and worked on St Paul's Cathedral with Sir Christopher Wren, though died before its completion. Strong left money in his will to the Barrington villages to build a stone crossing over the River Windrush, and stated that the bridge should be wide enough to allow two men to carry a corpse – presumably his – across in safety. Situated south of Bourton-on-the-Water and close to Great Barrington, Little Barrington is a special village not to be missed.

Uffington

The White Horse of Uffington is one of the most impressive sites close to the ancient Ridgeway path, which traverses the steep chalk downs brooding over the Vale of the White Horse. Other sites include Dragon Hill, The Manger, and Uffington Castle, which have been the subject of legend and folklore for over a thousand years

The White Horse of Uffington, with its elegant lines of white chalk bedrock, is thought to be the oldest hill figure in Britain. The image is a stylised representation of a horse (some would say dragon), some 374 feet in length, and is thought to date back as far as 1000BC in the late Bronze Age. Similar images have been found on coins from that period, and it is thought that the figure represents a horse goddess connected with the local Belgae tribe. The goddess is generally believed to be one form of Epona, worshiped throughout the Celtic world. The horse was ritually scoured every seven years under the jurisdiction of the local Lord, who had to fund the event. The festival – for that is what it became – could last for over three days, and consisted of fun and games, traditional cheese rolling, wrestling, and other pastimes. The focus of the games was in the enclosed earthen banks of Uffington Castle, an Iron Age hill fort, which the White Horse appears to be galloping toward when viewed from the air. Cheese rolling was held on the steep-sided valley known as The Manger, a strangely-shaped valley that folklore suggests was the supernatural grazing place for the White Horse, which would travel from its vantage point on the crest of the hill on moonlit nights. The festival, which may have had ancient origins, lapsed about a

hundred years ago, and it is fortunate that the White Horse did not become completely overgrown as a result. The horse is now cleaned by members of English Heritage, which is responsible for the site. Dragon Hill is a low, flat-topped mound situated in the valley below the White Horse. In legend, it is the place where St George slew the dragon, its blood spilling on the hilltop and leaving forever a bare white patch where no grass can grow. Some suggest that the horse is a representation of St George's steed, or even of the dragon itself.

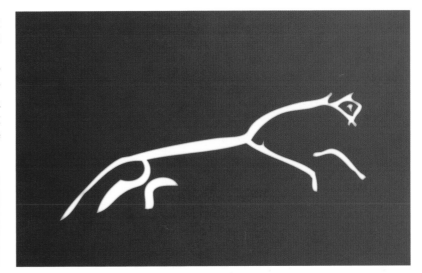

Directions to Uffington
A minor road off the B4507, opposite the turn-off to Uffington, leads to a car park, from which the sites can be explored

Ross-on-Wye

Perched on the banks of the River Wye, Ross-on-Wye is only a stone's throw away from and, unusually, is cited as the birthplace of the British tourist industry

From as early as 1745, the rector Dr John Egerton began taking friends on boat trips down the Wye valley from his rectory at Ross. The stunning riverside scenery, dramatic landscapes, abbeys and castles were all popular attractions for this new breed of tourist – or, as they were called back then – 'Seekers of the Picturesque.' The reason then, as is the reason now, is the Wye valley. This Area of Outstanding Natural Beauty (AONB) is an internationally important protected landscape straddling the borders between England and Wales, and one of the most dramatic and scenic landscape areas in southern Britain. The River Wye is the fifth-longest river in the United Kingdom. The upper part of the river passes through the settlements of Rhayader, near Builth Wells, and Hay-on-Wye, but the area designated as an AONB surrounds only the 72-mile stretch lower down the river, from just south of the city of Hereford to Chepstow. This area covers parts of the counties of Gloucestershire and Herefordshire. Limestone gorge scenery, and dense native woodlands, as well as wildlife, archaeological and industrial remains, make the area of special appeal to historians and naturalists alike, plus drivers, as the roads around here are superb, especially the A49 and the B4348, which takes you across the border to Abergavenny. From this twisting and undulating B-road, the Welsh hills loom before you, and in the rearview mirror, the landscape of England stretches back as far as the eye can see.

http://en.wikipedia.org/wiki/River_Wye
http://en.wikipedia.org/wiki/Rivers_of_Great_
    Britain
http://en.wikipedia.org/wiki/Rhayader
http://en.wikipedia.org/wiki/Builth_Wells
http://en.wikipedia.org/wiki/Hay-on-Wye
http://en.wikipedia.org/wiki/Chepstow
http://en.wikipedia.org/wiki/Gloucestershire
http://en.wikipedia.org/wiki/Herefordshire
http://en.wikipedia.org/wiki/Gorge

Malvern Hills

A source of great water, highly regarded by many, is one of the numerous reasons why the hills around Malvern hold great appeal

The Malvern Hills is one big ridge running roughly north to south, to the west of Great Malvern, which makes it quite easy to work out roughly where you are – most of the time! The area is very popular with walkers, and it's an opportune time to leave the car behind at the Red Lion pub on St Ann's Road at Great Malvern and head to St Ann's Well with its splendid café.

The café is set on the slopes of the Malvern Hills above Great Malvern, with commanding views eastward over the Severn flood plain. The building dates back to 1815, and houses an elaborately carved water spout and the infamous hostelry. The café provides vegan and vegetarian meals, teas, snacks, a selection of scrumptious cakes – plus you can also fill your glass with water fresh from the spring!

The northern half of the hills has the advantage of being easy to get off if you've had enough, and difficult to get very lost on, but this also means that you are rarely completely away from traffic noise (or perhaps that from the showground or, on Sunday afternoons, brass bands in Priory Park). The area immediately around the car park at British Camp (Wynds Point) can be particularly busy, thanks to the added attraction of a kiosk and hotel/pub providing a variety of food and drink. There's an easy access path starting from the car park just north of here (Black Hill), and, of course, the much steeper climb up British Camp itself.

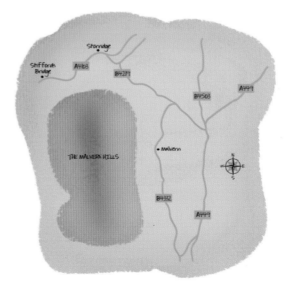

The Malverns stretch over three counties and are popular with walkers and cyclists. For the motorist, too, they are a visual spectacle and dominate the skyline from miles away.

Forest of Dean

The area is characterised by over 40 square miles of mixed woodland, and is one of the surviving ancient woodlands in England, originally reserved for royal hunting in 1066

Whilst today still a working, timber-producing forest, the Forest of Dean also faces many other pressures. It is, for instance, one of the oldest community forests in the country, with the towns of Coleford, Cinderford and Lydney situated at its periphery.

The Forest of Dean covers 35 square miles, and throughout you are welcomed by its custodian, the Forestry Commission, to explore, by walking the many miles of forest roads and tracks, or cycling the stone paved forest roads in the forest's centre. You will find a number of waymarked trails for cyclists and walkers across the forest, ranging in length from a few kilometres to long distance. There are plenty of picnic sites, car parks, and viewing points in the area.

For centuries, the forest was valued for its resources of iron, coal, stone, and timber. Today, it is a place of few crowds and great peace, with the largest area of old oak trees in Britain. It came to the Forestry Commission in 1924. To Dennis Potter, the famous playwright, who was born and grew up in the Forest, it was more than just a heart-shaped area on a map; for him, the beauty and magic of the landscape also captured his heart – as it will yours.

Directions to the Forest of Dean
The Forest of Dean district is located in the western part of Gloucestershire, close to the border with Wales, and is within easy access of the M4 (M48), M5 and M50 motorways, as well as many major roads

Exmoor & Dartmoor

Exmoor

Exmoor was designated a National Park in 1954. Although one of the smaller National Parks in England, it offers some great driving roads

The A39 is one of England's finest roads, and passes through some spectacular scenery, leading road-weary travellers to the tiny village of Porlock, nestling amongst the hills of north Exmoor, on the edge of a salt marsh separating the hills from the Bristol Channel.

Porlock itself is low-lying, but a steep climb up from the village in any direction will reveal spectacular views of the Bristol Channel and the South Wales coast beyond.

There have been human settlements at Porlock for thousands of years, and Stone Age remains have been found in the area. The village remains a vibrant local centre with numerous pubs and restaurants, at which can be sampled local fayre.

Samuel Taylor Coleridge was apparently interrupted by a man from Porlock whilst writing the poem *Kubla Khan,* and distracted to the point that he lost his inspiration and the work was never completed. This was explained away by the writer Douglas Adams, in *Dirk Gently's Holistic Detective Agency,* as a bid by one of the lead characters of the book to prevent Coleridge from discovering how to build a time machine in the late 18th century.

Two miles from Porlock lies Porlock Weir, where, on a clear day at low tide, you can occasionally see the remains of a prehistoric forest, in addition to the more obvious harbour. Porlock Hill is the steepest hill on an A road in Britain, climbing about 400 metres in two miles. It climbs in a westerly direction out of Porlock to a high plateau offering

views across Exmoor and the Bristol Channel. There's an alternative toll road, built in 1840 by the Lord of the Manor, which caravans and large vehicles are advised to use to avoid Porlock Hill. Even so, the Ship Inn at Porlock kept extra horses especially to help stagecoaches climb the perilous hill.

At 328 kilometres (204 miles) long, the A39 is one of Britain's longest roads (there are only nine longer A roads in the country), and runs from Bath to Falmouth, the majority of it forming the northern coast road of the south-west peninsula. The section of interest here is a 16-mile length from Minehead to Lynmouth, most of which runs through the Exmoor National Park.

Start just to the west of Minehead on one of the few upgraded sections of this part of the A39. Overtake slow lorries now in the third lane, as there won't be many chances during the rest of the trip.

At the top of the hill, the road reverts to two lanes and continues along a gentle grade as we pass turnings for Blackford and Selworthy.

Continue until you reach the edge of Porlock, where the road forks: the left-hand branch is one way downhill and takes the A39 down to Porlock; the right-hand road carries eastbound traffic.

Continue into Porlock, passing between stone walls on narrow streets. The main street has various 'touristy-type' shops, as well as a few pubs and restaurants. One of the hostelries is the Lorna Doone Hotel, which has a prime site on the main street.

This is where things really do begin to get interesting! Arriving at the bottom of Porlock Hill you will be presented with a choice of routes. My advice is to stay on the A39 by bearing left here, which will take you up the 1-in-4 Porlock Hill – it'll cost you nothing, but you've got a very steep climb ahead of you and it will put a smile on your face as you remember the horses of old, pulling carriages!

View over Parsonage Farm, Exmoor National Park, Somerset.

Directions to Porlock

Exit the M5 motorway at Bridgwater at J24, continuing on the A39, or exit the M5 at Taunton at J25 following the A358 to Williton and join the A39. The A39 will take you to Porlock

Best food/drink

The Ship Inn, High Street, Porlock, Somerset
TA24 8QD
Tel: 01643 862507

Relevant websites

http://en.wikipedia.org/wiki/Samuel_Taylor_
    Coleridge

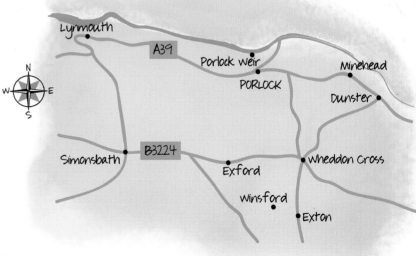

Dartmoor

One of England's wilder places, Dartmoor is famous for werewolves and war. The army uses the plains for training, and walkers enjoy the many paths and walkways to the various Tors. It's got a nice road, too ...

Unless you really want to get off the beaten track on unclassified roads, there's really just one main route that actually crosses the Park, as the main A30 skirts the north of Dartmoor and the A38 skirts the south.

The B3212 from Exeter will take you right across the middle of Dartmoor via Moretonhampstead. Many other smaller roads head off both north and south from here, but look out for road closures if the army is in town!

The B3212 runs west to Two Bridges from where you have a choice – either stay on this road to Yelverton, where you then drop down to Plymouth on the A386, cross the Tamar Bridge, then follow the A38 and A390 to the coast, or take the B3357 at Two Bridges to Tavistock, from where you follow the A390/A38/A390 to St Austell via Callington and Liskeard.

There is a tradition of military usage of Dartmoor dating back to the Napoleonic Wars. There's still a large army training camp at Okehampton – also the site of an airbase during the Second World War.

The Ministry of Defence (MoD) uses three areas of the northern moor for manoeuvres and live-firing exercises, totalling 108.71 square kilometres (41.97 square miles), or just over 11 per cent of the National Park. Red and white posts mark the boundaries of these military areas (shown on Ordnance Survey 1:25,000 scale maps). Flagpoles on many tors in and around the ranges fly red flags when firing is taking place. At other times, members of the public are allowed access. Blank rounds may also be used, but the MoD does not notify the public of this in advance – you have been warned!

Relevant websites
www.tripadvisor.co.uk/Tourism-g186254-Exeter_
    Devon_England-Vacations.html
www.tripadvisor.co.uk/Tourism-g315958-
    Moretonhampstead_Dartmoor_National_Park_
    Devon_England-Vacations.html
www.tripadvisor.co.uk/Tourism-g551654-
    Two_Bridges_Dartmoor_National_Park_Devon_
    England-Vacations.html
www.tripadvisor.co.uk/Tourism-g315961-
    Yelverton_Dartmoor_National_Park_Devon_
    England-Vacations.html

Clapperbridge, near Postbridge, Dartmoor.

Devon & Cornwall

Hartland Quay

One of the best stretches of coastline in the whole of England, Hartland Quay makes a great day out for all the family

Hartland Quay was once a thriving harbour, mainly because of the area's remote location and the difficulty of transporting goods by road. In the mid 18th century, once the railway had reached Bideford and improvements were made to the road network, the harbour fell into decline,and it became uneconomic to repair from the repeated storm damage.

From Hartland Town the road winds down and round past Hartland Abbey, and on through the small hamlet of Stoke, home to the impressive Church of St Nectan that towers above the parish. Eventually, the road comes to an end and a small kiosk can be seen on the left. This is the entrance to Hartland Quay. In the holiday season (Good Friday until the end of the October half term), and weather permitting, this kiosk is manned from 10am until 5pm. There is a small car parking charge which entitles you to park all day. There is a steep tarmac road so you can drive all the way down; ideal for families with young children or anyone who has difficulty walking back up. If you prefer a leisurely stroll down and carry a camera, you will be rewarded with plenty of photo opportunities as Bideford Bay and the famous jagged Hartland rock formations come into view. There is another car park and grassy picnic area about halfway down.

For over 400 years Hartland Quay has been a haven for mariners and travellers in fair weather or foul. The old 16th century quay has long since gone, but a visit to the Shipwreck Museum will reveal the mysteries of how this historic quay worked in bygone days: the geology and natural history of this dramatic part of the Atlantic Heritage Coast is fascinating and well documented here. The museum also displays photographs, paintings and relics that bring to life stories of derring-do, smugglers, shipwrecks, fishing, and coastal trade and industry.

When the tide is out the beautiful sheltered cove contains some interesting rock pools, and a sandy beach that can be easily reached via the slipway. Enjoy safe bathing, fishing, surfing and exploring. Twenty minutes' walk south of Hartland Quay is Spekes Mill Mouth, the most spectacular waterfall on the North Devon Atlantic Heritage Coast. It's also just a short walk to Blackpool Mill Cottage, setting for the BBC's adaptation of *Sense and Sensibility*.

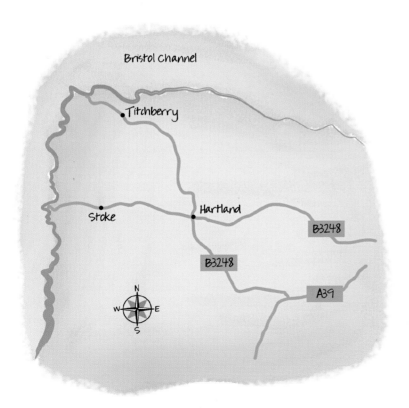

Hartland Point is one of the most unspoilt parts of the UK, with stunning views out to sea, and miles of superb, undulating coastline.

Directions to Hartland Quay
Hartland is approximately 14 miles west of Bideford and 15 miles north of Bude on the A39 Atlantic Highway

Best food/drink
The Anchor Inn, Fore Street, Hartland, North Devon EX39 6BD
Tel: 01237 441414

Relevant websites
http://www.thenorthdevonfocus.co.uk/spekesmill.htm

Following page: A lone lighthouse stands as a sentinel over the Cornish coastline, serving to warn ships of the treacherous rocks below the waterline.

Page 55 image: Tin mines dot the coastline around Cornwall, a reminder of a once thriving industry that served the world.

Cornish coast

With its whitewashed seaside villages and greener-than-green countryside dotted with Celtic ruins, the Cornish peninsula is a hybrid of historical attractions and natural beauty

While some of Cornwall's main routes are two-lane, be prepared for narrow roads for most of your journey. When you tire of driving, park your car for a while and explore the tiniest of hamlets and coves by walking along some of the 630-mile South West Coastal Path, the longest footpath in Britain.

Begin your tour in Penzance with a visit to the 9th century Penzance Cross, one of Cornwall's most famous Celtic crosses, located outside the Penlee House Gallery and Museum. From here, drive some three miles east to St Michael's Mount, which, throughout history, has been a tin-trading post, pilgrimage site, and military fortress. Climb to the top of the island's castle and visualise the approaching ships of the Spanish Armada. To your east is the Lizard Peninsula, blessed with fine beaches and some of the best pasties in Cornwall. To your west is Penwith Peninsula, dotted with Neolithic sites, and Mounts Bay. At low tide, you can walk right out to St Michael's Mount via a causeway. When the water is up, opt for a short ferry ride from Marazion.

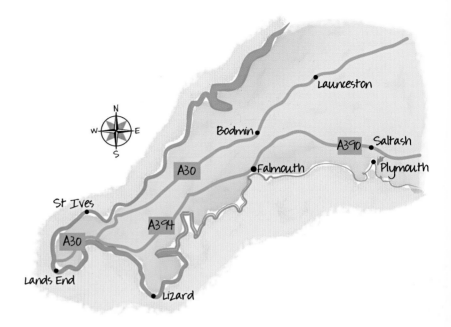

Relevant websites
www.penleehouse.org.uk

Best food/drink
Morrab Road, Penzance
Tel: 01736 363625

The many bays around Bude provide the weary motorist with visual feasts. And it's a feast of a foodie kind; refreshments are never far away!

Following pages: Waiting for the tide. Sunsets in Cornwall are always spectacular.

St Michael's Mount

The jewel of Cornwall, St Michael's Mount is just reward for a trip to the coast in this part of England

St Michael's Mount has been associated with religious worship from the 12th century, when a Benedictine monastery was erected here, although legend and conjecture suggest that the Mount has been regarded as a place of spiritual importance long before that.

St Michael's Mount is thought to have been the site of a tin port in the late Iron Age, just before the Roman Invasion. The importance of the mount as a place of pilgrimage traditionally dates back to the 5th century, when a group of people had a vision of St Michael over the mount (the legend is somewhat garbled, and the vision has been attributed to various groups of people). It was this event, however, that is supposed to have given the Mount its archangel dedication, although this may date to much later when the Benedictine monastery was founded. The Mount is also associated with St Keyne, who traditionally blessed a stone seat with the power to grant dominance in marriage, depending on who out of the happy couple managed to sit on it first!

A Benedictine monastery was built here in 1135, which was a dependency of Mont St Michael in Brittany, and lasted until the dissolution of the monasteries by Henry VIII in the 16th century. One interesting story suggests the bones of a giant man were discovered when the church was rebuilt in the 14th century, after an earthquake destroyed the original structure. The remains of the monastery were rebuilt into a castle, home of the St Aubyn family from the 17th century, and now owned by the National Trust.

St Michael's Mount was once known as Cara Cowze in Clowze, or The Hoar Rock in the Wood, which is considered by some to be a folk memory of when the sealine was not so far inland, and the area was covered in woodland. The lore was most probably passed on from written records when the mount was a monastic settlement linked with Mont St Michael in Brittany. St Michael's Mount is also not far from the legendary lost land of Lyonesse.

The Mount was also the legendary abode of the giants Cormoran and his wife, Cormelian. Jack the giant killer eventually defeated Cormoran, after the giant terrorised the surrounding lands.

St Michael's Mount is also the starting point for the infamous St Michael's ley, a broad line linking the Mount, St Michael's Church Brentor, St Michael's Church Burrowbridge, St Michael's Church Othery, St Michael's Church, Glastonbury Tor, and Stoke St Michael.

One of the most noteworthy points of interest on St Michael's Mount is an underground railway, which is still used to transport goods from the harbour to the castle. Tin miners built it in around 1900, replacing the pack horses previously used. Due to the steep gradient, it cannot carry passengers.

Directions to St Michael's Mount
The Mount can be reached at low tide from Marazion off the A394: in good weather there's also a ferry service at high tide

Best food/drink
Hotel Penzance, Britons Hill, Penzance, Cornwall TR18 3AE
Tel: 01736 363117

Relevant websites
http://en.wikipedia.org/wiki/St_Michael%27s_Mount

Dorset & Somerset

Durdle Door

Durdle Door is one of the most photographed landmarks along the Jurassic Coast of Dorset, and well worth a visit

Along with Dover's white cliffs, Dorset's Durdle Door and Lulworth Cove are synonymous with all that is England.

The famous rock arch in the sea was formed as a result of the softer rocks being eroded behind the hard limestones, allowing the sea to punch through them.

The name Durdle is derived from the old English word 'thirl,' meaning bore or drill. Eventually, the arch will collapse to leave a sea stack such as those that can be seen at Ladram Bay in East Devon. But let's hope you manage to get there before it does!

Each year more than 200,000 walkers use the footpath between Lulworth Cove and Durdle Door, making it the busiest stretch in the southwest. Below the cliffs lies a sweeping beach that was once three separate coves. This popular beach has no facilities, although there are public toilets at Durdle Door Holiday Park. In summer, a mobile kiosk on the path leading to Durdle Door provides ice creams and other refreshments.

Scenes from the 1967 film of Thomas Hardy's novel *Far From the Madding Crowd* were filmed here, and in 1997 parts of the film *Wilde*, starring Stephen Fry, were also shot here. Many may also recall Cliff Richards' 1990 hit *Saviour's Day*, which had Cliff singing down on the beach and on the clifftop in its promotional video. Later, the group Tears for Fears shot parts of its video for *Shout* at this iconic arch.

Durdle Door is privately owned by the Welds, a family that owns 12,000 acres in Dorset in the name of the Lulworth Estate.

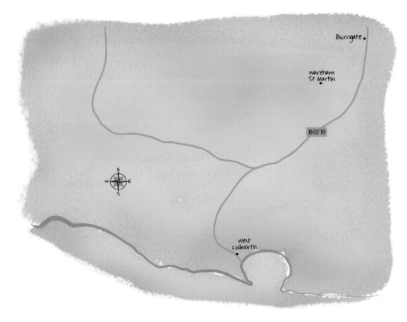

Best food/drink
The Weld Arms, East Lulworth, Wareham, Dorset BH20 5QQ Tel: 01929 400211

Relevant websites
http://en.wikipedia.org/wiki/Lulworth_Estate

The name Durdle is derived from the old English word 'thirl,' meaning bore or drill.

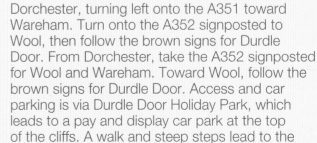

Directions to Durdle Door
From Bournemouth, take the A35 toward Dorchester, turning left onto the A351 toward Wareham. Turn onto the A352 signposted to Wool, then follow the brown signs for Durdle Door. From Dorchester, take the A352 signposted for Wool and Wareham. Toward Wool, follow the brown signs for Durdle Door. Access and car parking is via Durdle Door Holiday Park, which leads to a pay and display car park at the top of the cliffs. A walk and steep steps lead to the beach

The beech avenue near Kingston Lacy is a grand introduction to the house to which it leads. The name of Kingston Lacy comes from its ancient lords, the Lacys, Earls of Lincoln, who held it together with Shapwick and Blandford. After the destruction of the family seat at Corfe Castle, a new home site was chosen on the Lacy Estate by Sir John Bankes. However, the house was eventually paid for and finished by his son, Ralph.

The original house was designed by Sir Roger Pratt, and built between 1663 and 1665, with interiors influenced by Inigo Jones, but executed by his heir, John Webb. For many years, the house was believed to have been entirely constructed by Jones, for it so resembled his work, until the plans of Webb were discovered. It is a Grade I listed building, and houses a great collection of paintings and other works of art.

69

The Mendips and Somerset

Situated only 20 miles or so from the famous city of Bath, the Mendip Hills area is steeped in history and legend associated with Roman and Iron Age remains, and features some of Somerset's most attractive landscapes

This apparently modest range of limestone hills stretches about 50 miles from the coast at Weston-super-Mare, almost to Frome in the east (the Mendip Way long-distance footpath covers this route, and is an ideal focus for a short-break holiday).

The summits of the Mendips offer spectacular, panoramic views over the Bristol Channel, and toward Exmoor. The folds in the hills have created many attractive valleys in which mellow, stone-walled villages nestle. Underground, the Mendips are honeycombed with caverns, carved out of the limestone rock by the erosive power of water over millions of years. Some caverns, such as Wookey Hole caves, have long been popular visitor attractions, but many more are known only to experienced cavers. Nearby are the magnificent landscape features of Cheddar Gorge and Burrington Combe.

Evidence of man's former settlements and industries abounds on the Mendips. These include Neolithic earthworks, Bronze Age barrows, Iron Age hill forts, and lead mining remains dating from Roman times to the 19th century.

So, where does the name 'Somerset' come from?

The 'Sumorsaete' recorded in the Anglo-Saxon Chronicle and remembered in the motto of Somerset County Council were, so the language experts tell us, 'the people of the summer lands.' The Welsh/ Celts, who were here before the Saxons, called the area Gwlad yr haf, which means 'land of summer.' It seems that the Saxons invading these parts later in the 7th century described the area as the native Celts did before them.

The sun shining on the bright green spring grass of the Levels can be seen clearly from across the Bristol Channel, and is, perhaps, the image which so struck those who lived here long ago. Acres of green marshlands spreading far inland meant that the winter floods were over and rich summer grazing would soon be available. It was the land that came into its own in the summer, and the name the new owners gave to their principal settlement was, appropriately, summer town: Somerton.

Wells is an unspoilt market town of outstanding beauty, located in rolling countryside, at the foot of the Mendip Hills. Steeped in history, it is England's smallest city, and one of the most beautiful. Although much of Wells' glory lies in the past, it is very much a present-day city; a busy market town, and an educational and commercial centre.

Directions to Wells
A371 south-east from Cheddar, A371 west from Shepton Mallet, A39 north from Glastonbury

Best food/drink
The Fountain, 1 St Thomas Street, Wells, Somerset BA5 2UU Tel: 01749 672317

Relevant websites
http://www.touruk.co.uk/somerset/som_ched.
   htm
http://www.touruk.co.uk/somerset/som_shepton.
   htm
http://www.touruk.co.uk/somerset/som_glast.htm

Wells Cathedral dates primarily from the late twelfth and early thirteenth centuries, and is a spectacular example of Gothic architecture.

Staffordshire

The Roaches

Like a gigantic mouthful of teeth chewing away at the Peak District, the tangled rock escarpment of The Roaches forms one of the most dramatic higher landscapes in Britain

The Roaches, along with Hen Cloud and Ramshaw Rocks, form a gritstone escarpment that marks the southwestern edge of the Peak District. Best viewed from the approach along the Leek road, they stand as a line of silent sentinels guarding the entrance to the Peak District, worn and scuplted into fantastic shapes by the elements.

The area is one of rock and heather which once belonged to the Swythamley Estate. Following the break up of this estate, the area – including the Roaches and Hen Cloud (some 975 acres) – was purchased in 1980 by the Peak District National Park Authority in order to protect this unique environment and guarantee access for the public.

Hen Cloud is an impressive, solitary edge that rises steeply from the ground. The Roaches have a gentler approach, and actually consist of two edges – lower and upper tiers – with a set of rock steps connecting them. Built into the rocks of the lower tier is Rock Cottage, a tiny, primitive residence that was once home to the gamekeeper, now converted to a climbing hut. Below and to the west of the main edge is a line of small subsidiary edges known as the Five Clouds.

This area was once famous for its wallabies, which had been released from a private zoo at Swythamley during World War II, and had managed to breed and survive until the late 1990s, when the last individuals seem to have disappeared.

The entire area is a favourite spot with walkers and rock climbers, and the edges provide some of the best gritstone climbing in the country, with famous classic routes such as Valkyrie, the Sloth, and the Swan. In some ways, the locality has become a victim of its own popularity as it is very busy at weekends.

The Roaches, along with Ramshaw Rocks and Hen Cloud, form a gritstone escarpment that is very popular with hikers and climbers. It is often very busy, especially at weekends.

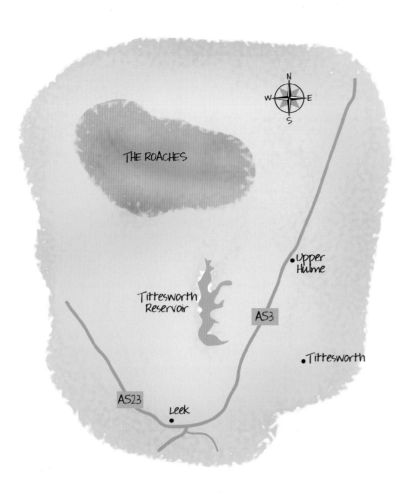

THE ROACHES

Upper Hulme

Tittesworth Reservoir

A53

Tittesworth

A523

Leek

Directions to The Roaches
Turn off the A53 Buxton-Leek road on the steep hill at Upper Hulme. Pass through the village and turn off to cross the stream and go through the works. Continue along the narrow road until you see the crags. Park along the road

Best food/drink
Rock Inn, Upper Hulme, Leek, Staffordshire ST13 8TY Tel: 01538 300324

Relevant websites
http://en.wikipedia.org/wiki/Gritstone)
http://en.wikipedia.org/wiki/Escarpment
http://en.wikipedia.org/wiki/Hiking

Wiltshire

Wiltshire

Once the most pot-holed county in England, Wiltshire nevertheless contains many great views to greet the inquisitive driver

As classic English counties go, Wiltshire surely is up there with the best. And, uniquely, I've taken this opportunity to include a road that you will have to walk, rather than drive.

The Ridgeway is an ancient trackway described as Britain's oldest road. At 85 miles (137km), the route follows the chalk hills between Overton Hill near Avebury, and Ivinghoe Beacon in Buckinghamshire, and represents part of a route in use since Neolithic times. Specifically, the Ridgeway hugs the ridge tops of open downland west of the Goring Gap and the tree-covered Chiltern Hills, east of the River Thames, thus avoiding once-difficult woods and marshes in the valleys below.

For at least 5000 years, travellers have used the Ridgeway. Originally connected to the Dorset coast, the Ridgeway provided a reliable trading route to The Wash in Norfolk. The high, dry ground made travel easy and provided a measure of protection by giving traders a commanding view that could warn of potential attacks. The Bronze Age saw the development of the White Horse, along with the stone circle at Avebury. During the Iron Age, inhabitants took advantage of the high ground by building hill forts along the Ridgeway to help defend the trading route.

Following the collapse of Roman authority in Western Europe, Saxon and Viking invasions of Great Britain saw the Ridgeway used as a road for moving armies. In medieval times, the Ridgeway was used by drovers, moving their livestock from the West Country and Wales to markets in the Home Counties and London. Prior to the Enclosure Acts of 1750, the Ridgeway existed as an informal series of tracks across the chalk downs, chosen by travellers based on path conditions. Once enclosures started, the current path developed through the building of earth banks and the planting of hedges. Since 1973 the Ridgeway has enjoyed the status of a National Trail.

Maybe one of the more unique pubs in Wiltshire is the Poplar Inn at Wingfield, outside Trowbridge, which has its very own cricket club; the fixture timetable is to be found on the website. Apart from entertaining cricket lovers, the inn provides a wide and varied choice of food and drink, and specialises in catering for weddings and other special events.

And on the subject of pubs, one of the oldest in Wiltshire is the George Inn at Lacock in the north of the county. The tiny village of Lacock (three miles from Chippenham) is totally unique in that it is

When Stonehenge was first opened to the public it was possible to walk around and even climb on the stones, but the stones were roped off in 1977 as a result of serious erosion. Stonehenge is now a World Heritage Site, and visitors are no longer permitted to touch the stones, though are able to walk around the monument from a short distance away.

owned by the National Trust, which has carefully preserved the village look. However, it is a 'living village,' with a thriving community and village school. The George Inn is a family-run pub with happy and friendly staff who can be relied on to provide the best service, food and drink to their many visitors, no matter how busy they are.

Another family-run pub is the Horseshoe Inn at the village of Mildenhall, close to Marlborough. The pub is set in an area of outstanding beauty in over one acre of ground. In the family for several generations, the pub was extensively renovated around 10 years ago and boasts open fires, oak beams, and a welcoming atmosphere.

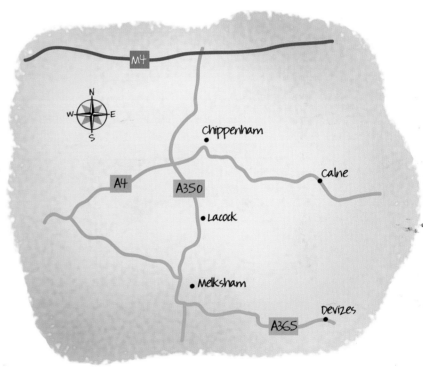

The Westbury white horse is the oldest of the Wiltshire horses. It lies on Westbury Hill, on the edge of the Bratton Downs, immediately below the Iron Age hill fort called Bratton Camp, northeast of Westbury and near to the villages of Bratton and Edington. There is a car park with a viewing point on the B3098 just east of Westbury.

Relevant websites

http://en.wikipedia.org/wiki/Ancient_trackway
http://en.wikipedia.org/wiki/Chalk
http://en.wikipedia.org/w/index.
    php?title=Overton_Hill&action=edit&redlink=1
http://en.wikipedia.org/wiki/Avebury
http://en.wikipedia.org/wiki/Ivinghoe_Beacon
http://en.wikipedia.org/wiki/Buckinghamshire
http://en.wikipedia.org/wiki/Neolithic
http://en.wikipedia.org/wiki/Goring_Gap
http://en.wikipedia.org/wiki/Chiltern_Hills
http://en.wikipedia.org/wiki/River_Thames
http://en.wikipedia.org/wiki/Dorset
http://en.wikipedia.org/wiki/The_Wash
http://en.wikipedia.org/wiki/Norfolk
http://en.wikipedia.org/wiki/Uffington_White_
    Horse
http://en.wikipedia.org/wiki/Bronze_Age
http://en.wikipedia.org/wiki/Avebury
http://en.wikipedia.org/wiki/Iron_Age
http://en.wikipedia.org/wiki/Hill_forts
http://en.wikipedia.org/wiki/Roman_Empire
http://en.wikipedia.org/wiki/Viking
http://en.wikipedia.org/wiki/Anglo-Saxons
http://en.wikipedia.org/wiki/Medieval)
http://en.wikipedia.org/wiki/Drover
http://en.wikipedia.org/wiki/West_Country
http://en.wikipedia.org/wiki/Wales
http://en.wikipedia.org/wiki/Home_Counties
http://en.wikipedia.org/wiki/London
http://en.wikipedia.org/wiki/Inclosure_Acts

Directions to Lacock

Leave the M4 motorway at Junction 17 and take the Chippenham road (A350). Continue through Chippenham and head toward Melksham. There is a left-hand turning for Lacock

Best food/drink

The George Inn, 4 West Street, Lacock, Chippenham SN15 2LH Tel: 01249 730263

Lacock village is preserved by the National Trust and is a magical step back in time, as well as a place of worship for lovers of photography. It was here, in 1835, that William Henry Fox Talbot made his first image, signalling the birth of photography.

Yorkshire & Lancashire

Brimham Rocks

Located within the Nidderdale Area of Outstanding Natural Beauty, Brimham Rocks is a collection of strange rock formations spread across 50 acres

Geologists believe that the majority of these enormous millstone grit boulders owe their bizarre shape to the natural erosion that occurred during and after the last glacial period, or Ice Age, in Britain. Owned and managed by the National Trust, Brimham Rocks offers visitors the opportunity to rock climb on formations such as the Dancing Bear, the Druid's Writing Desk, and Idol Rock, and to enjoy majestic views of the surrounding countryside. The rocks are also the perfect base from which to explore approximately 400 acres of naturally beautiful, wildlife-rich woods and moorland.

While it is true that Brimham Rocks is a desirable location for experienced rock climbers and those who enjoy guided country walks, it's also a wonderful place for the less adventurous. Locals and tourists alike come to Brimham Rocks to enjoy leisurely strolls, family picnics on the grounds, or simply take photographs of the awe-inspiring rock formations and scenery. You are allowed to climb on the rocks, but it's advised that all individuals, especially those with young children, do so with caution, as they can be extremely dangerous. All in all, a trip to North Yorkshire would be incomplete without taking the opportunity to see and experience these wondrous geological formations.

The site is typically open from 8am to dusk, year-round. It is important to note that, particularly during good weather, Brimham Rocks can be quite busy. Therefore, be prepared for limited availability in terms of parking, and, possibly, long queues at the entrance. Also, parking fees apply for visitors who are not members of the National Trust.

Dogs are permitted at Brimham Rocks, but must be kept on a lead during the months of April, May, and June in order to protect the ground-nesting birds.

A free geological exhibition is offered at the Brimham House for visitors who are interested in learning more about the history of Brimham Rocks. It is also the location of a small National Trust gift shop, a refreshment kiosk, and restroom facilities.

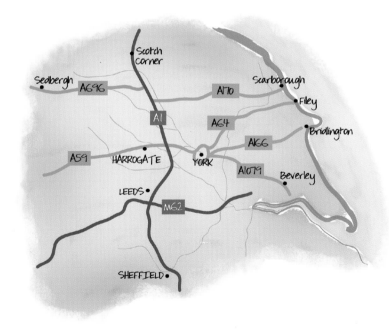

Previous three pages: the curious rock formations at Brimham in Nidderdale are scattered over some 50 acres on Brimham Moor.

Directions to Brimham Rocks
Brimham Rocks is located 4 miles east of Pateley Bridge off the B6265, 10 miles south west of Ripon, and 11 miles north west of Harrogate off the B6165

Best food/drink
The Yorke Arms, Ramsgill, Pateley Bridge, North Yorks HG3 5RL
Tel: 01423 755243

Relevant websites
http://1-800-www.helium.com/items/1510777-travel-destinations-brimham-rocks-north-yorkshire

Wensleydale

Swaledale has the River Swale, Wharfedale has the Wharfe, and Ribblesdale has the Ribble. Yet – strangely – there's no River Wensley in Wensleydale …

Wensleydale, perhaps best known for its cheese, made famous by the *Wallace and Grommit* animations, is formed by the River Ure – sometimes pronounced Yore – and rises high in the Pennines in the vicinity of Hawes village.

Hawes derives its name from 'Hause,' meaning a narrow neck of land. It is located at the southern end of the Buttertubs Pass, a natural route with a steep roadside drop that unnerves many motorists. The pass links Wensleydale to Swaledale in the north, and the limestone features hereabouts are said to resemble tubs of butter.

Fossdale Beck is one of the streams that feed the River Ure at Hawes. It rises on Great Shunner Fell and, further down its course, pours over a limestone cliff to form a 30-metre single drop waterfall to rival High Force in Teesdale. This is the Hardraw Force, or the Scaur, as it is also known, one of the most famous sites of Wensleydale. It may not be the biggest, or most powerful waterfall in England, but it's certainly the highest single drop fall in England. The word Force, incidentally, derives from Fors, a Viking word for a small waterfall.

Hawes is the home of the creamery responsible for production of Wensleydale Cheese. It is said that French monks, who settled at Fors near Aysgarth further down the dale, in 1145, brought cheese-making to Wensleydale. The monks later moved to a new site in Wensleydale at Jervaulx, but took their cheese-making skills with them. After dissolution of the monasteries during the reign of Henry VIII, the cheese-making skills passed into the hands of local farmers, and, in the nineteenth century, were eventually inherited by the present cheese factory at Hawes.

East of Hawes, the River Bain at Bainbridge joins the River Ure from the south. In historic times this was located within the forest of Wensley, and was used as a hunting park by the lords of Middleham Castle. A Shrovetide horn-blowing ceremony at Bainbridge dates to the time when hunters were guided back to the safety of the village by the blowing of a horn.

The Romans had a lookout station close to Bainbridge, on a hill at nearby Addleborough, and an ancient British chieftain is said to be buried in a cairn close by. Further up the Bain is Semer Water, a small lake, which, according to legend, once drowned the villagers of Bainbridge after they refused charity to a beggar.

Across the other side of the river from Addleborough is Askrigg, a Viking place name that means 'the ridge where ash trees grew.'

Wensleydale was the home of the Metcalfes, one of Yorkshire's most famous clans, after it migrated from Dentdale. The Metcalfe Society holds records dating back to the 14th century, when Metcalfes began living in the area.

It later became an important market town in the dale, and a market charter was granted in 1587. The neighbourhood of Askrigg was traditionally the home of the Metcalfe family, who lived at nearby Nappa Hall. The hall was built in 1459 by a James Metcalfe to protect against the raids of marauding Scots – a frequent problem for Wensleydale. Mary Queen of Scots was imprisoned in Nappa Hall, before she was moved down the dale to Castle Bolton. The property is an impressive example of a fortified 11th century house.

Four miles east of Askrigg is the village of Carperby, its name deriving from Caipere, an old Irish moniker. 'By' is the Viking word for settlement, so the founder of this place was probably of mixed Irish/Viking descent. Irish Vikings arrived in the dales and vales of northern Yorkshire via the Viking colony of Dublin, from which they were evicted in the 10th century: they seem to have constituted an important element of Yorkshire's population in the Viking period.

Aysgarth, on the opposite side of the river to the south, is, of course, famed for its falls; a series of waterfalls stretching over a half-mile section of the River Ure. The falls occur in three stages – upper, middle and lower. Aysgarth is yet another Viking name, deriving from 'Ayks kerth,' meaning a gap in the hills where oak trees grew. It is one of the most beautiful spots in Yorkshire.

Wensley village to the east of Aysgarth gives its name to the whole of Wensleydale. Most Yorkshire Dales are named after their rivers, but, for some reason, Wensleydale is named after a village.

Wensleydale's river is the Ure – an old Celtic name related to the Gaulish river Isura. In Anglo-Saxon times, Wensley village was called Woden's Ley (after the pagan god Woden), and is thought to have been the site of a pagan shrine.

Directions to Wensleydale
Take the A1 north to Leyburn, then follow the A684 est to Hawes, some 8 or so miles away

Best food/drink
The Black Swan, Fearby, Masham, Ripon, North Yorkshire HG4 4NF
Tel: 01765 689477

Relevant websites
http://en.wikipedia.org/wiki/Dentdale

Ribblehead Viaduct

A spectacular testament to man's engineering prowess, the Settle to Carlisle railway has at its heart a jewel of a bridge that makes for a stunning view, from train and from car!

Some 26 years ago the Settle-Carlisle Railway seemed doomed to close, one reason for which was that the Ribblehead Viaduct was said to be beyond economic repair. Happily, this was not so, the viaduct was restored, and the line was saved.

The 24-arch Ribblehead Viaduct stands boldly in the stunning landscape of the Yorkshire Dales, a tribute to the 200 people who died during its construction, and that of nearby Blea Moor Tunnel.

There are two ways of seeing the viaduct – from the hills and dales and from the train, from which you may be lucky enough to see the shadow of the viaduct stretching for up to a mile as the sun sets below Chapel le Dale, the last resting place of those who died.

Designed by the engineer John Sydney Crossley, the first stone was laid on 12 October 1870, and the last in 1874. It is 104 feet (32m) high and spans 440 yards (402m).

The viaduct is curved, and so may be seen by passengers on the train. The train journey itself from Settle to Carlisle is short enough to allow the Yorkshire Dales holidaymaker to take a return day trip (steam-hauled, in the tourist season) which will include a few hours in the border town of Carlisle.

Two thousand navvies building the viaduct established shanty towns on the moors, naming them after victories of the Crimean War, sarcastically, for posh districts of London, and from the Bible. There were smallpox epidemics, and deaths from industrial accidents, necessitating that the church graveyard at Chapel-le-Dale be extended.

The Settle & Carlisle line is one of three north-south main lines, along with the west coast main line through Penrith, and the east coast main line via Newcastle. British Rail attempted to close the line in the 1980s, citing the reason that the viaduct was unsafe and would be expensive to repair. A partial solution was to single the line across the viaduct, preventing two trains from crossing simultaneously. The closure proposals generated tremendous protest, and were eventually retracted. The viaduct, along with the rest of the line, was maintained, and there are no longer any plans to close it.

The viaduct is Grade II* listed and a Schedule D Ancient Monument.

Ribblehead Viaduct is just over the border from Cumbria into North Yorkshire. Hundreds of railway builders (navvies) lost their lives constructing the line, from a combination of accidents, fights, and smallpox outbreaks.

Directions to Ribblehead Viaduct
Some official parking available near the road junction of the B6255 and B6479.mPlease do not park on road verges, or drive down the access track to the viaduct

Best food/drink
The Station Inn, Ribblehead, Nr Ingleton, North Yorkshire LA6 3AS
Tel: 01524 241274

Relevant websites
http://www.absoluteastronomy.com/topics/Settle
http://www.absoluteastronomy.com/topics/
      Carlisle_railway_station
http://www.absoluteastronomy.com/topics/
      Yorkshire_Dales
http://www.absoluteastronomy.com/topics/Navvy
http://www.absoluteastronomy.com/topics/
      Shanty_town
http://www.absoluteastronomy.com/topics/
      Crimean_War
http://www.absoluteastronomy.com/topics/
      Smallpox
http://www.absoluteastronomy.com/topics/
      Epidemic
http://www.absoluteastronomy.com/topics/
      Chapel-le-Dale
http://www.absoluteastronomy.com/topics/West_
      Coast_Main_Line
http://www.absoluteastronomy.com/topics/
      Penrith,_Cumbria
http://www.absoluteastronomy.com/topics/East_
      Coast_Main_Line
http://www.absoluteastronomy.com/topics/
      Newcastle_upon_Tyne
http://www.absoluteastronomy.com/topics/
      British_Rail
http://www.absoluteastronomy.com/topics/
      Scheduled_Ancient_Monument

Trough of Bowland

The Trough of Bowland is Lancashire's 'hidden gem.' This beautiful region remained largely inaccessible to the casual tourist until well into the 20th century

The Forest of Bowland, also known as the Bowland Fells, is a region of barren gritstone fields, deep valleys, and peat moorland, mostly in northeast Lancashire. A small part extends to North Yorkshire, and much of the area was historically part of the West Riding of Yorkshire. In 1964 it was designated an Area of Outstanding Natural Beauty, and is used for grouse shooting, walking, and cycling, though it is relatively unfrequented by tourists.

One of the best-known features is Pendle Hill, which is separated from the main part of the Forest of Bowland by the Ribble Valley.

Much of the Bowland region is designated a Site of Special Scientific Interest for its important areas of heather moorland and blanket bog. Nationally and internationally important for its upland bird populations, the hen harrier is the region's symbol. There are over 500 listed buildings and 18 scheduled monuments within the Trough of Bowland, too.

'Forest' is used in its traditional meaning of 'a royal hunting ground,' and much of the land still belongs to the British Crown as part of the Duchy of Lancaster. In the past, wild boar, deer, wolves, wild cats, and game roamed the forest.

Heather moorland on Clougha, in the northwest of the Forest of Bowland, is a remainder of the ancient wilderness that once stretched over a huge part of England, encompassing the Forest of Bowland, Sherwood Forest (Nottinghamshire), the New Forest (Hampshire), and Savernake Forest (Wiltshire).

The hills on the western side of the Forest of Bowland attract walkers from Lancaster and the surrounding locality. Overlooking Lancaster is Clougha Pike, the westernmost hill. The hills form a large, horseshoe shape with the open end facing west. Clockwise from Lancaster are Clougha Pike (413m/1354ft), Grit Fell (468m/1535ft), Ward's Stone (561m/1840ft), Wolfhole Crag (527m/1729ft), White Hill (544m/1784ft), Whins Brow (476m/1561ft), Totridge (496m/1627ft), Parlick (432m/1417ft), Fair Snape Fell (510m/1673ft), Bleasdale Moor (429m/1407ft), and Hawthornthwaite fell (478m/1568ft).

The area is home to the geographic centre of Great Britain, which is close to the Whitendale Hanging Stones, around four miles (6.4km) north of Dunsop Bridge.

The Forest of Bowland hosts an annual challenge event – the Bowland Challenge – in which teams of walkers navigate a series of grid references over a ten-hour period. Proceeds from the event go to support Bowland Pennine Mountain Rescue Team.

Best food/drink
Pendle Inn, Barley, Burnley, Lancashire BB12 9JX
Tel: 01282 614808

The Bowland region of Lancashire is a quiet oasis away from the industrial north, and well worth a detour from the M6 at Preston.

Directions to the Trough of Bowland

From Yorkshire follow the A65 from Skipton; just after Ingleton turn left and follow the motorway and Lancaster signs (A687, becoming the A683 just before Melling).
Continue following signs for the motorway and Lancaster until you come to the village of Caton

Woodhead Pass

Taking you across the roof of England, from Barnsley to Sheffield, is the legendary Woodhead Pass. Great views are guaranteed

Forming one of two routes connecting Manchester with Sheffield, the A628 Woodhead Pass carries a very high traffic volume, including huge numbers of trucks, plus local and long-distance cross-country traffic. The other road, the A57, is no longer signed as a through route between Sheffield and Manchester, so the A628 gets the bulk of this traffic.

The height and exposure of the road often creates problems during bad weather, and the road is sometimes closed due to snowfall or high winds, so if you're off for a winter drive, check first! Traffic passes within six feet of front doors in places, and the almost complete absence of pavement is a hazard for pedestrians.

Leaving Tintwistle through a short section (with a 40mph speed limit), the views become increasingly dramatic over Longdendale,

Directions to Woodhead Pass
The road starts to the east of Manchester at the end of the M67 motorway and A57

Best food/drink
Dog and Partridge Country Inn, Bordhill Flouch, Sheffield, South Yorkshire S36 4HH
Tel: 01226 763173

Relevant websites
http://www.sabre-roads.org.uk/wiki/index.
   php?title=A57
http://www.sabre-roads.org.uk/wiki/index.
   php?title=NSL
http://www.sabre-roads.org.uk/wiki/index.
   php?title=A616
http://www.sabre-roads.org.uk/wiki/index.
   php?title=M1
http://en.wikipedia.org/wiki/Manchester
http://en.wikipedia.org/wiki/M67_motorway

Low cloud, billowing up from the valleys, and cresting over the A628 Woodhead Pass at twilight. Meanwhile, the traffic, oblivious to the scene, threads its way through the frosty landscape.

the character and appearance of which changes in differing weather and light conditions. The speed limit increases to the national limit, and the next nine miles through the dale are mostly uphill around a seemingly never-ending series of bends. Some are broad, others are at right-angles complete with numerous warning signs, red road markings, and even cats eye-type reflectors on the crash barriers to highlight the edge of the road (and the sometimes 80-foot drop-off on the other side!).

The route passes Bottoms, Valehouse, Rhodeswood, Torside, and Woodhead reservoirs as you continue to climb. This section can be tortuously slow if stuck behind a fully-loaded truck, as there are very few places to overtake, and not even any lay-bys for lorries to pull over into and let traffic behind them clear.

The stone-arched Woodhead Bridge takes you across an arm of Woodhead reservoir, though the arches are all but submerged when the water is at its highest level.

You then pass (at long last!) a lay-by carved out of the cliff face – usually chock-a-block with trucks as they pause for breath and a bacon buttie. There is a long-standing memorial to a mountain biker who was killed here, which always has flowers and cycling trophies on it. Other accident damage is usually visible throughout this part of the route, generally in the form of knocked-down walls on or near bends.

The road then becomes slightly straighter and steeper, and the drop-off on the right – into what is now a ravine – gets deeper as you near the top, passing a couple more lay-bys. Crossing Salters Brook Bridge brings you at last into South Yorkshire, before you reach the windswept summit at 442 metres (1450 feet), some 314 metres (1030 feet) above where you started out in Hollingworth. This height and exposure means that winter weather is often problematic, and Woodhead Pass often features prominently in radio travel bulletins.

A straight section leads into the descent on the east side, which is much shorter and steeper, and the lucky people travelling the other way have a crawler lane to pass the vast number of trucks. A new alignment takes you away from Flouch and its mini island, and instead around a newer one, the junction with the A616. The bulk of the traffic turns right here, and continues towards the M1 and Sheffield, the once strong industrial heart of England.

Surrey & South East

London at night is a visual feast of colour and activity, and, despite the congestion charge, worth a drive after the rush hour when darkness descends and traffic becomes a tad more manageable. The route from Westminster, along the Embankment to St Paul's Cathedral, is definitely worth a try – and don't forget to take your camera with a tripod for those long exposures!

111

Thaxted Mill

Built in 1804, and put to use for a hundred years, John Webb's windmill is a tower mill, the only remaining windmill in Thaxted, as well as the largest and most advanced of all the Thaxted mills. Built to satisfy a growing demand for flour at a time of agricultural expansion, it was constructed from local materials, the bricks made and fired half a mile away in the Chelmer Valley. John Webb owned the farmland on which the mill was built

A gallery at first floor level surrounded the mill, and was used for easy loading and unloading from carts and wagons, but when the mill was first built it was from this gallery that the sweeps (the sails), were individually adjusted to suit the wind (this was when spring sails were fitted). Later, these were replaced with patent sails and thereafter all four sails could be adjusted at the same time by using an invention known as a 'spider,' which is a centrally controlled system of levers. By 1907, the mill was uneconomic to work, and when offered for auction it failed to sell. For years it was a playground for local children, until, in the 1930s, repairs were carried out so that it could be used as a scout and youth centre. By the late 1950s, it was again derelict and in need of repair, and so it remained until 1970 when a Trust was formed to restore the building and open it to the public as a rural museum. Restoration work has been carried out in stages, and in 1991 the sails were re-erected and turned for the first time in almost 85 years. In 1996, one set of stones was restored so, once again, it can claim to be a working mill capable of grinding grain into flour. Since restoration work started, well over £100,000 has been spent, around 70 per cent of which has been raised by open days and fund-raising, the balance coming from various grants. The museum has developed greatly and covers a wide range of exhibits, and is an added attraction for visitors to the mill. Although the mill is owned by the Parish, restoration has been made possible through the enthusiasm of many volunteers, and by the support of many visitors.

Directions to Thaxted Mill

From the M11, leave at the Birchanger Green Services exit and head East on the A120 to Great Dunmow. From there head north following the signs for Easton Lodge Gardens and follow the B184 to Thaxted

Essex coast

The Essex coast is often maligned, but actually harbours some beautiful locations

If in search of the traditional pleasures of the seaside with a modern twist, the Essex coast is the perfect location. From award-winning beaches and unspoilt coastlines, to picturesque villages and the historic port of Harwich, it's one of England's more archaic – yet still enjoyable – areas. Steeped in history and popular with Londoners looking to get away for the day, a gentle amble around the B1032 and surrounding roads will throw up some surprises. The capital of the 'Essex Sunshine Coast,' Clacton is a popular seaside town with tree-lined streets, sand/shingle beaches (Blue Flag and Quality Coast Awards), and beautiful clifftop gardens. The fun-packed 19th century pier offers fairground rides and sea fishing. Why not try out a range of watersports, or enjoy an evening out at one of the two theatres? The town centre boasts a range of shops, restaurants, pubs and clubs for all ages.

With a reputation as an exclusive resort, Frinton retains the atmosphere of the 1920/30s. Tree-lined avenues sweep down to the elegant esplanade and cliff-top greensward, with its colourful, Victorian-style beach huts. The sandy beach (Quality Coast Award) is quiet and secluded, and best enjoyed with a cream tea! Walton-on-the-Naze is a family seaside resort, with sandy beaches, seafront gardens and quaint narrow streets. The pier is the second longest in England, offering fairground rides, ten pin bowling and sea angling. Just to the north is The Naze, an unspoilt headland of heath, saltmarshes and sandy beaches – although its 70 feet high cliffs are gradually eroding away.

The walled town of Petworth reverberates to the sound of expensive car exhausts every July when the Goodwood Festival of Speed comes to town, further down the A283.

Petworth is mentioned in the Domesday Book, and is, perhaps, best known as the location of Petworth House, the grounds of which (known as Petworth Park) are the work of Capability Brown. The house and its grounds are now owned and maintained by the National Trust.

Another historic attraction in the town, Petworth Cottage Museum in the High Street, is a monument to domestic life for poor estate workers in the town in about 1910. At that time the cottage was the home of Mrs Cummings, a seamstress, whose drunken husband had been a farrier in the Royal Irish Hussars, and on the Petworth estate. The railway line between Pulborough and Midhurst once had a station at Petworth, but this was closed to passenger use in 1955, and finally to freight in 1966, though the station building survives as a bed and breakfast establishment.

Petworth fell victim to bombing in World War II on 29 September 1942, when a lone German Heinkel HE-111, approaching from the south over Hoes Farm, aimed three bombs at Petworth House. They missed the house, but one bounced off a tree and landed on Petworth Boys School, and some 28 boys lost their lives, along with the headmaster, Charles Stevenson, and assistant teacher, Charlotte Marshall.

Surrey is oft overlooked as a destination in favour of the more popular coastal attractions further down the A3 and M3 motorway routes. But a detour to Box Hill, or even the countryside surrounding Guildford, is well worth the effort to see unspoilt rural scenes and delightful village pubs.

121

Directions to Bodiam Castle

Nearest major road is A21. Turn left, off the A21, 2 miles south of Hurst Green. Follow the signs from there

One of the most famous and evocative castles in Britain, Bodiam was built in 1385, as both defence and comfortable home. The exterior is virtually intact, the ramparts rising dramatically above the moat. Enough of the interior survives to give an impression of castle life: there are spiral staircases and battlements to explore, and wonderful views of the Rother Valley from the top of the towers. In the impressive gatehouse is the castle's original wooden portcullis, an extremely rare example of its kind in Britain.

Lincolnshire, Northamptonshire & Norfolk

Lincolnshire coast

One of the quieter counties, Lincolnshire nevertheless boasts some of the best roads – and superb beaches for a day at the sea

It's the largest agricultural county in England, stretching from Humberside in the north to Norfolk in the south, and one steeped in history, from the Roman occupation to King John losing the Crown Jewels in The Wash.

The name 'Lincoln' is derived from the Roman word for the occupation of the site around the Brayford area – Lindum Colonia. Today, the southern part of Lincolnshire is renowned for its farmland and growing large amounts of wheat, barley, sugar beet, oilseed rape, cabbages, potatoes, cauliflowers, and onions. The land is flat fenland and the soil rich in nutrients, thanks to thousands of years of retreating sea and marshland. There are many small, quaint market towns dotted about, and all are well worth including in your drive around the county.

The northern part of Lincolnshire is a hidden jewel of glorious rolling countryside, excellent for driving, and known as the Lincolnshire Wolds. The city of Lincoln is situated here, in an elevated position where the Wolds begin, with the Cathedral jutting into the sky, dominating the countryside.

If it's a jaunt to the coast you're after, head for Skegness with its amusements, leisure activities and beaches. Also popular are the resorts of Mablethorpe, Cleethorpes, Ingoldmells, and Chapel St Leonards. Caravan sites on the Lincolnshire coast are abundant, too, if you want to tow your home comforts along.

The port of Grimsby used to be famous for its fishing industry, though now more oil tankers than fishing boats can be seen. There is a large refinery nearby at Immingham to which the tankers deliver their crude oil, and from where we get our petrol, delivered by numerous tankers.

Nature and wildlife are attractions for many Lincolnshire-bound tourists: the south east of the county is mainly fenland which draws many species of birds, and a visit to one of the nature reserves (Gibraltar Point, Saltfleetby, and Threddlethorpe) is highly recommended. A native seal colony at the Donna Nook reserve gives the opportunity of superb glimpses of the grey seal.

Those born in Lincolnshire are sometimes given the nickname of Yellowbellies (often spelt 'Yeller Bellies,' to reflect how it might be pronounced by a Lincolnshire farmer). The origin of this term is debated, but is most commonly believed to derive from the uniforms of the 10th Regiment of Foot (later the Lincolnshire Regiment), which had very bright yellow panels on the red coats for identification on the battlefield.

At the turn of the 20th century, several large engineering companies materialised in the county to support the mechanisation of the agricultural industry (the industrial revolution). Most famous, perhaps, is Fosters of Lincoln, which built the first tank.

Lincolnshire's transport links are poorly developed compared with many other parts of England. The road network within the county is dominated by single carriageway A roads and local roads (B roads), as opposed to motorways and dual carriageways – in fact, Lincolnshire is one of the few UK counties without a motorway, and, until a few years ago, it was said that only about 35km (22 miles) of dual carriageway existed in the whole of Lincolnshire. The M180 motorway passes through north Lincolnshire, splitting into two dual carriageway trunk roads to the Humber Bridge and Grimsby, and the A46 is now dual carriageway between Newark and Lincoln.

A famous Lincolnshire person is Margaret Thatcher, first female Prime Minister of Britain; she was born in Grantham and served her constituents there for the entirety of her time in government. Lincolnshire is also home to the world-famous RAF display team The Red Arrows whose base is at RAF Scampton just outside Lincoln.

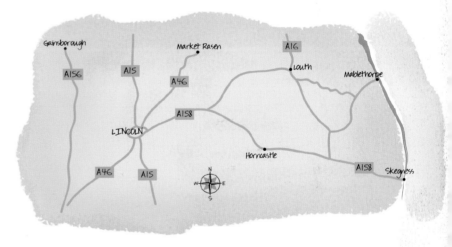

Directions to Lincoln
From the A1, exit at Newark and follow the A46 all the way to Lincoln. You'll see the cathedral against the horizon

Best food/drink
The Victoria, 6 Union Road, Lincoln, Lincolnshire, LN1 3BJ Tel: 01522 541000

Lincoln Cathedral dominates the skyline from your approach on the A46 and can be seen from up to 20 miles away. It is one of the most important Medieval cathedrals in Europe.

Following page: The Wolds, near Tetford, Lincolnshire.

Northamptonshire

A little-known village on the border of Northamptonshire and Rutland is the setting for a pretty remarkable piece of engineering ...

Harringworth is a beautiful stone village set in the Northamptonshire countryside, just on the Rutland border. Nearby facilities include various fishing and shooting opportunities, Rutland water, Rockingham speedway, and the market towns of Uppingham and Oakham. There are several popular local attractions such as Rutland County Museum at Oakham (an ironstone building originating from 1794), Oakham Castle, and Barnsdale Gardens – home to the late Geoff Hamilton of BBC2's *Gardener's World* fame.

Harringworth Viaduct, also known as Welland Viaduct or Seaton Viaduct, crosses over the River Welland between Harrington in Northamptonshire, and Seaton in Rutland. Its impressive span of 82 arches stretch for three quarters of a mile and, having been completed in 1878 by the Midland Railway, it is over 132 years old. With its impressive length, Harringworth Viaduct is the longest masonry railway viaduct across any valley in Britain, and carries a Grade II Listed Structure status.

Situated on the Oakham to Kettering line, the viaduct carries double track across its entire length; however, the line was only lightly used up until February 2009 as a diversionary route for East Midlands Trains and special excursions. Since February 2009, a daily service has operated between St Pancras and Corby, and soon this service will be extended to Melton Mowbray, meaning the viaduct will once more experience daily services passing across it.

The best view of the impressive viaduct can be witnessed from

the Seaton side of the valley looking south east. This can make an impressive late afternoon shot with Harringworth village and the church spire as an ideal backdrop. Many local footpaths around the village of Harringworth lead underneath the striking structure, and one of the best to take is the river footpath that can be found 500 yards north of the village.

If you happen to be visiting Northamptonshire, a trip to Harringworth Viaduct is highly recommended. Best to go on an afternoon, though, if you're after a series of shots; too early and it's difficult to find the best location to shoot from for sun position.

Viewed from the Wakerley road, the Harringworth Viaduct crosses the magnificent Welland Valley towards Seaton, a small village perched atop the hill overlooking the county of Rutland.

Directions to Harringworth
Take the A427 towards Rockingham, the A6003 through Caldecott, and then the B672. Follow signs to Harringworth and Seaton Road (main road through village). From the A1 take the A47 towards Leicester, then the B672 (signposted Caldecott) and follow signs to Harringworth

Best food/drink
The White Swan, Harringworth, Seaton Road, Harringworth, NN17 3AF
Tel: 01572 747543

North Norfolk coast

North Norfolk embraces around 400 square miles, and is one of the most beautiful coastlines in the UK

You don't have to travel far in Norfolk to come across pretty villages, bustling market towns, secluded sandy beaches, and acres of unspoilt countryside.

North Norfolk's coastline stretches for 43 miles, much of it is designated as an Area of Outstanding Natural Beauty. The diverse landscape includes wide sandy beaches, pine forests, salt marshes and mudflats, and, as the seasons change, the countryside displays very different qualities.

North Norfolk is famous for its long, white, sandy beaches such as those at Holkham, Wells and Brancaster: the setting for pop videos, movies – and lots of happy family days out. The wide beaches are washed by safe, shallow waters, perfect for sunbathers, swimmers, and those looking for plenty of space to play.

Further along the coast, Mundesley is a Blue Flag beach where children can paddle safely in tidal pools. The pebbly beach at Sheringham has also won a Blue Flag award for its cleanliness.

As you drive along the North Norfolk coast road you are bound to discover your own favourite beach, and that's the real beauty of the area – the freedom to stop wherever you want and just get out and walk.

Directions to Cromer
Take the M11 towards Cambridge. From Cambridge, take the A14 towards Norwich, then the A11 until you reach the Norwich Outer Ring Road. Follow the directions from Norwich to Cromer

Best food/drink
Tuddenham Mill, Tuddenham, Nr Newmarket, Suffolk IP28 6SQ
Tel: 01638 713 552

Every year during the winter the A1101 – the main road to Welney in Norfolk – is flooded for days at a time, as the Old Bedford River and the Hundred Foot Drain fail to cope with the level of rain draining from the Fens. Understandably, the residents of Welney aren't entirely happy about this: the floods pretty much prevent anyone from visiting their village, and they are irritated by the 45-mile detour needed to go around the floods to reach the road to Ely.

North Norfolk has some wonderful and picturesque towns and villages that are perfect for a day out, or as the base for your holiday in the county.

Cromer and Sheringham have been popular seaside resorts for almost 200 years, and offer a relaxed pace of life for those looking for a really laidback holiday. Both towns have a Blue European Flag for their clean beaches and safe bathing waters.

Blakeney, Cley and Wells are outstanding centres for wildlife, and paradise for birdwatchers. You can take a boat to Blakeney Point to see the seals, or try crabbing on the quayside.

Holt is a small Georgian town that's a great place for shopping, or browsing the many art and crafts galleries. You won't be able to resist the tempting cafes and speciality food shops …

Walsingham is known all over the world as a pilgrimage centre for people of many faiths. There are several religious buildings in the pretty village, and the peaceful atmosphere makes Walsingham a perfect spot for those who want to escape for a while, the hustle and bustle of the larger resorts.

North Norfolk forms part of the largest coastal nature reserve in England and Wales. Bitterns and terns, oystercatchers, avocets and marsh harriers are among the many species that make North Norfolk a prime site for bird-watching enthusiasts.

The Peddars Way is probably one of the most famous paths in the UK. It starts from Thetford and, as it approaches the coast at Holme Next the Sea, becomes the Norfolk Coast Path. The route runs all the way to Cromer, with several optional detours on the way. Walking along the path is a wonderful way to see the North Norfolk countryside from a different perspective, if you want to leave the car behind. The Norfolk Wildlife Trust's reserve at Holme Dunes is one of the area's most attractive landscapes, and the combination of mudflats, sand dunes, salt marsh and redbuds give it a real air of mysticism. It is an important bird-watching site, where a huge variety of species – including avocets, ringed plovers, redshanks, curlews and lapwings – can be spotted. Holme Dunes is another key site for winter wildfowl.

At Salthouse Marshes, further along the coast, a shingle bank protects the coastal grazing marshes and salt water lagoons from the voracious appetite of the North Sea. Bird-watchers can look out for black-tailed godwits, ruffs, redshanks and snow buntings, as well as several thousand brent geese in the winter months.

For those seeking sophisticated exclusivity, the villages of North Norfolk, including Burnham Market, Blakeney and Cley Next the Sea, offer stylish shops and award-winning restaurants. Slightly further afield, at the gateway to Thetford Forest, is Tuddenham Mill, a 200-year-old granary now converted into one of the most beautiful restaurants in the area, with boutique-style rooms, and self-contained apartments in the grounds.

Often referred to as 'Chelsea on Sea,' North Norfolk has become a popular destination for the sophisticated London set, and has many celebrity fans. In the numerous restaurants, cafes, boutiques and galleries you will find fine food, beautiful clothes, art and gifts to rival the best Covent Garden has to offer.

Tips for great travel pictures

The skill involved in visualising and predicting a photograph before you stop the car and reach for the camera is as key to your success as the craft itself

When was the last time you knew you had taken a truly great photograph? Last week? Last year? $\frac{1}{60}$ sec ago? For many photographers, lured away from the emotive side of imaging to the techo-obsessed culture of computers, the craft of putting a picture together in the mind's eye is lost until the download.

"Photographers will soon become mere camera operators," the late Patrick Lichfield once said to me. "The real skill and the real art of a great image will soon lie in the hands of the computer expert." A scary thought, but he had a point. In this golden age of photography, where we as 'camera operators' still retain control, it's up to us to make sure we know exactly what we want at the time in which we take it – before the development, and definitely before the download …

The mind's eye

Whilst reading this, pause for a moment and consider what motivates you to take photographs in the first place … As photographers, we are acutely visually aware, and while some of us know exactly how sharp our skills are, many others don't. 'Seeing' an image should be an instinctive process; framing a scene in your mind before reaching for the camera should be something you get into the habit of doing every time you look for a picture. Even when simply walking down the street or sitting in the garden at home – get into the habit of looking for pictures. Photographers never switch off!

So, what to look for? There are three components behind every good image – the holy trinity of photography, if you like – and they are line, tone, and shape. Line can be anything from the walls of a building to the wrinkles on a face; tone brings these to life, while shapes are the jigsaw pieces that join them together. Work these three ingredients into your picture and you're halfway there. Get the framing right and – bingo – it's time to grab that camera!

So, framing, then: how do you know when you've got it right? To understand this, you need to start thinking in rectangles. Psychologists have found that the human eye interprets an image by working from the bottom left to the top right. What you need to do as a photographer is adapt your thinking to accommodate this psycho-philosophy. "There are always two people in every picture: the photographer and the viewer," said the great landscape photographer Ansel Adams. And he was right. Your job is to provoke the viewer. And there are tricks to help you do this.

Steam boat 'Gondola,' Coniston Lake.

Judging potential

A photograph should evoke some kind of feeling or emotion in the viewer. That's the point of any visual display – to engage and provoke. Subject matter, naturally, plays a very big part in this, and while some areas of photography are more dramatic to work in than others, there are certain rules and mechanics that neatly translate across all disciplines, the principle one being composition. Whilst the rule of thirds is well known and well used, it shouldn't be taken as gospel that you must compose to its preset guidelines. It's true that the eye looks for balance in a picture, and the rule of thirds helps you achieve that, but there's the rub: as a photographer you are looking for a reaction all the time in your work, be it appreciation or abject horror. And one way to unsettle the viewer is to offer them an image that is harder to interpret. It's the principle of framing. Artists do it all the time. Look at the past masters for reference: Salvador Dali, Picasso, MC Escher … photographers such as Man Ray, Henri Cartier-Bresson, Bill Brandt and David Bailey were (and are) exponents of the great and noble art of provocation.

Tell a story

Images are narrative by nature, particularly travel images. They inform, define and determine a viewer's perception of places and events. A change of lens or a change of angle is sometimes all it takes to influence interpretation.

An image is powerful only if a viewer feels involved with it. This is why documentary photographers prefer small cameras such as the Leica Rangefinder. Their diminutive size and wide optics mean that you have to be up close and personal with your subject. Proximity, don't forget, is directly proportional to impact.

When composing a photograph, look for the details and concentrate on the edges of the frame, ensuring that the main part of the picture – the focal point – is strong enough to engage the viewer. Eyes are always the best means of capturing a viewer's attention: on a psychological level there is nothing better than a pair of pupils staring back at you – and visually they are the areas of highest contrast, which therefore attract the most attention.

Compare and contrast

Which brings us to contrast, itself a very important part of narrative imagery. Contrast is used as a way of guiding a viewer from one part of an image to another. Traditionally, monochrome photographers used it to help guide and shape a viewer's interpretation, and perception of a scene. Ansel Adams invented the Zone System of exposure precisely for this reason – to tackle exposure and produce the optimal reading, taking into account a subject's tones and contrast.

Lighting is very much part of your gameplan. There's a famous photography quote that goes something like this: "Colour photography records the colour of a subject's shirt. Black & white records the colour of its soul." It's an anonymous quote but whoever said it really had the medium nailed. Shadows and contrast are the strengths of a monochrome image, and should always be exploited for maximum impact. A subject stands or falls by the way it reacts to light. A red filter in front of the lens will beef up your clouds and send those blue skies black to dramatic effect, whilst faces react best to an orange filter, which reduces freckles and skin blemishes.

Of course, it's all so much easier now that the digital age is upon us, but that's not to say that we shouldn't misunderstand traditional principles. The art of seeing is all about recognition: observing the moment and knowing how to record it creatively and with impact.

Seeing is believing

We are all connected emotionally with what we see. Either through a lens or through our eyes, regardless of subject, we perceive it through our own unique psychological filter that subconsciously assesses a scene's appeal in neutral terms.

We cannot change this element of visualisation; it's what makes us all unique as people and, of course, photographers. When the matter of committing a scene to film or card arises, our brain has already done most of the hard work for us. All we have to do is follow that most basic of human abilities – instinct – and reach for the camera.

Let your senses do the work

Photography is information. As photographers we are imparting this data in visual terms, and how we show it determines its interpretation.

Most photographers have an idea of what their chosen subject is before they reach for their camera. Research is a critical part of the creative process, and can have a decisive effect on how a subject is tackled. Wildlife photographers, for example, are experienced zoologists and know their subjects inside out. Think about it: would you know the best way to photograph a funnel-web spider without getting bitten? Or how about the best way of approaching a wild elephant? Okay, you won't find many of these wandering down Croydon High Street, but I'm sure you take my point – it's all about knowledge. In the same way that mountaineers study maps before setting off to conquer a peak, so you must study your subject before embarking on your journey with a camera.

For the keen motorist-photographer, you will have a degree of control on the events you intend to document. Interpretation, therefore, will rest upon your creative choices; choices that rely as much on technique as they do on equipment selection.

Let's examine some popular travel subjects and study the best ways of photographing them.

Architecture

If you've tried your hand at architectural photography you've probably come across the effects of perspective. Photograph the front of a building and you'll see that the top of it looks narrower than the base, which gives the impression that the building is leaning away from you. Move into a more confined space where you have to point the camera upward slightly, and the effects become even more pronounced. It's a real problem, but what's the solution? Well, one way round it is to tackle it straight on – use the problem of perspective distortions to exaggerate the effect. Make tall buildings look even taller! This dodge is particularly useful – and often the only solution – where space is tight, and you don't have the opportunity to step backward to get a better view.

Landscapes

There are two separate issues here; what time of year and what time of day you photograph a scene. The same scene will produce dramatically different photographs as the seasons come and go, yet many of us only ever take pictures outdoors in the height of summer, when the blue skies and verdant foliage offer a riot of bright, saturated colours, resulting in uniformly vivid, crisply contrasty photographs of every scene. The truth is that, photographically speaking, shooting in the middle of a hot summer's day may be the easiest option, but it's also going to produce landscapes lacking any subtlety or atmosphere. This is partly down to light quality on such days; the high sun and bright sky produce a very flat illumination of the scene, and a cloudless sky – even if it is a beautiful deep blue – lacks any drama or visual interest of any description. That's not to say you shouldn't shoot in the summer, just don't forget the huge photographic opportunities offered during the rest of the year.

The time of day that you take your picture is just as important as the time of year, especially in the summer when light quality in long days varies enormously from dawn to dusk. Almost without exception, the best time to photograph is within an hour or so of sunrise or sunset when the sun is still relatively low in the sky and – during the winter months – shadows stretch across scenes, adding interest to even the most mundane tableau. The colour of light starts with warm orange tones, cools down as noon approaches, and begins to warm up again as the day draws to an end. We've all seen beautiful dawn and dusk skies from our hotel rooms; the dedicated landscape photographer will be sitting waiting for the perfect moment to take a picture. Wherever your travels take you, make sure you set the alarm for just before sunrise at least once; not only will you be rewarded with stunning light and the possibility of a truly dramatic sky, you'll also be able to photograph even the most popular places at the one time they aren't crawling with other people. And exactly the same goes for the evening just before sunset – pick up your camera and go for a wander one night instead of heading straight for the bar. This is especially true in beach resorts: beaches are not that interesting, photographically, until they empty of people, and the light takes on an almost magical quality as the sun sets.

Family portraits

Take pictures regularly so that you, your family, and friends can see how much your children have changed. Capture your kids setting off for the first day of school each year. Or mark their growth against a tree as you watch them and the tree grow.

Be patient. Don't expect to get the perfect family shot immediately. Sit back and wait for the right moment, then shoot quickly. Shoot at eye level, as eye-to-eye contact is as engaging in a picture as in real life. Try sitting on the ground and snapping some photos from the child's perspective. If you want some added drama, shoot from below the subject looking up to give the subject a greater air of dominance in the frame.

Arch detail, Stamford.

When photographing older family members, watch for reflections in glasses. A slight turn of the head might just get rid of an unwanted highlight, and could save you loads of retouching time!

Always engage your subjects by talking to them, keeping their faces animated and alive. Natural expressions – rather than forced smiles – will always look better in pictures.

Use a long lens (or the long end of your zoom) to home in on candid moments, and choose a shallow depth of field to focus maximum attention on the subject.

Spend a maximum of an hour and a half on a portrait session with children, because of their limited attention spans.

For children, start off with very simple compositions, and focus on big eyes looking into camera. Then move on to simple poses, and try to capture the subject moving or interacting with a sibling.

Wildlife

Jaw-dropping animal pictures don't happen by accident, but are the result of careful preparation, and more than a few sleepless nights.

Ask any wildlife pro, and they'll quickly tell you the only way to get good pictures of a subject is to understand it. And that's as true for birds in your back garden as it is for antelopes in Africa. Getting close to your subject – no matter how big or small – requires specialist knowledge, and specialist kit.

Approach your subject with a firm plan, and a clear objective. If you arrive at a location not knowing what you want, you will waste valuable time and, more importantly, risk disturbing your subject in your efforts to choose the right lens and get your plan into action.

The right equipment is vital if you're going to have any chance of success. Obviously, a long lens is going to significantly increase your chances of getting a great picture, but there are other key factors which can also get you closer to the action.

Pay attention to your appearance: no, I don't mean don your Sunday best! Don't use scented soap or aftershave or perfume, and wear clothes that don't rustle and have no shiny bits on them, which could glint in the sun and reveal your location to the subject you're trying to get closer to.

Once you know the exact habits of your quarry, including where and when it's likely to be at any given time, you can begin to plan your photograph. Don't just turn up at the location and expect to get the shot of your dreams, either. Give your subject time to get used to your presence and your camera gear. The easiest way of doing this is to erect a camouflaged hide and allow your subject to become familiar with your daily routine. After about a week, your subject will have become used to your presence, and your success rate will greatly improve.

Of course, the closer you can get to your subject, the more scope you will have over lens choice. If you're shooting a fledgling emerging from its nest, for example, you could use a wide-angle lens, which has loads more depth-of-field than a standard lens or zoom, and which could provide you with a whole new angle on your subject.

Pay attention to shadows and use their power to strengthen your image. Control contrast with contrast filters on the lens (if you are using film), or later in Photoshop's in Channel Mixer.

Conclusion

Whilst the craft of shooting pictures may be second nature, the art of seeing the picture first can be harder than it looks. Practice, careful study of other photographers' methods, more practice, followed by more study, will help shed light on how to be a more intuitive image-maker.

Camera equipment is not the be-all and end-all, and it's easy to become distracted by the myriad of functions and modes on today's cameras.

The purity of an image is more or less proportional to the purity of the photographer's vision. And it's that vision that you need to hone in order to rise from being just another photographer to someone a bit special.

Good luck in your journey ...

Dos and don'ts

Do
• Spend time researching your location, observing how the light falls on it and when the best time of day is for the best shadows and texture
• Watch the weather forecast the day before you plan to shoot to make sure your journey isn't a wasted one
• Seek permission from landowners before you walk into fields, and respect property and areas of outstanding natural beauty
• Respect the environment!

Don't
• Go out without a tripod; your three-legged friend will allow you to shoot with a slower shutter speed and thus a smaller aperture for maximum sharpness
• Just use one lens. Experiment with different focal lengths and camera angles to ensure you get the most from a scene
• Leave litter or gates open

Describes in a clear, friendly manner everything today's driver needs to know about choosing and using a car in an economical and eco-efficient way. The book explains what matters most to the car buyer when optimum fuel economy and lowest emissions are priorities, and why four-wheel-drive and automatic transmission present challenges to eco-friendly driving.

Highly detailed advice on driving for best fuel economy is supplemented by helpful information on alternative fuels, hybrid powertrains, and much more. Featuring a thorough examination of the advantages and disadvantages of the most promising fuels of the future – electricity and hydrogen – this is essential reading for the modern driver.

Paperback • 14.8x21cm • £9.99 • 96 pages • 32 colour pictures • ISBN: 978-1-845843-51-9

*p&p extra. Call 01305 260068 for details. Prices subject to change.

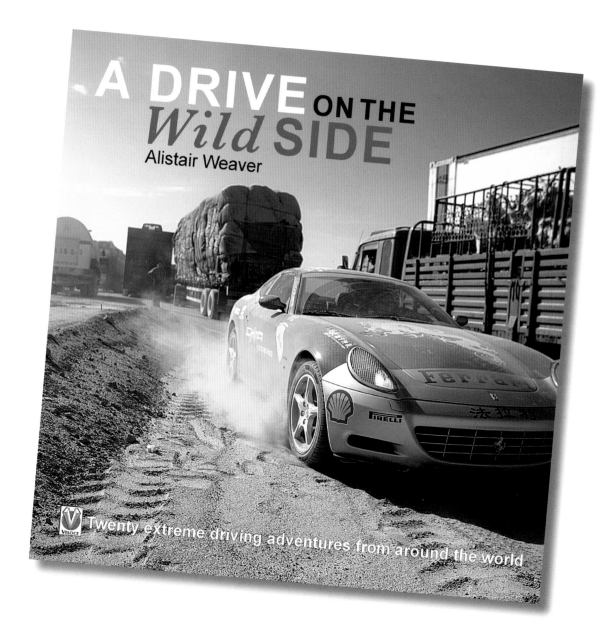

Written by award-winning journalist and television presenter Alistair Weaver, and illustrated by some of the world's leading automotive photographers, A Drive on the Wild Side, takes you on an extraordinary journey along some of the world's most challenging roads. Experience the heat of the Laos jungle, the loneliness of the Arctic, and the bullet-marked streets of Beirut from behind the wheel of some of the world's finest cars. Find out what it's really like to drive a Ferrari 612 across the forgotten wastelands of western China, or to chase poachers on the slopes of Mount Kenya. This book recounts the fascinating, hair-raising and moving stories experienced during a career of automotive adventure, helped by 400 stunning photos. This book will appeal to car and travel enthusiasts across the world.

Hardback • 25x25cm • £12.99 • 176 pages • 341 pictures • ISBN: 978-1-845841-00-3

*p&p extra. Call 01305 260068 for details. Prices subject to change.

Index